KU-048-490

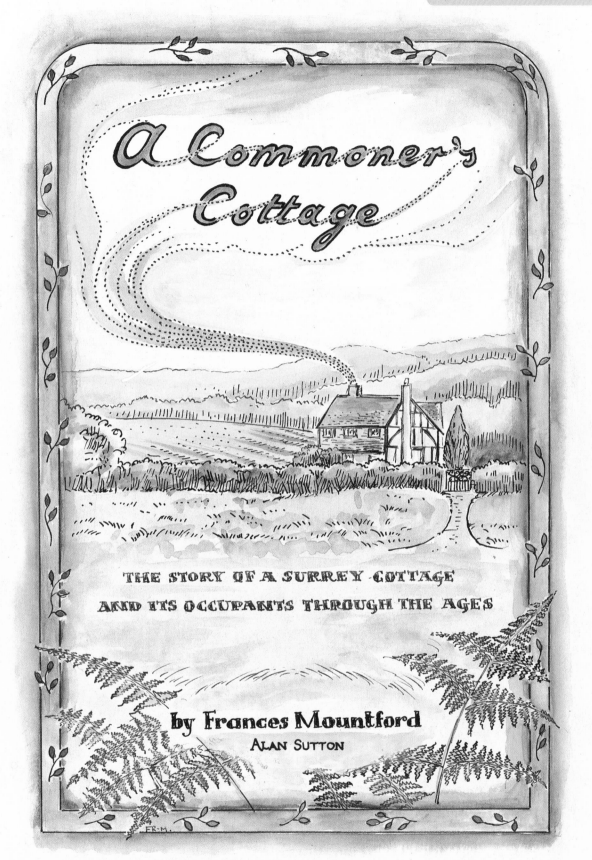

A Commoner's Cottage

THE STORY OF A SURREY COTTAGE AND ITS OCCUPANTS THROUGH THE AGES

by Frances Mountford

ALAN SUTTON

First published in the United Kingdom in 1992
Alan Sutton Publishing Limited • Pheonix Mill • Far Thrupp • Stroud
Gloucestershire

Reprinted 1995

First paperback edition 1995

Reprinted 1996

Copyright © Frances Mountford, 1992

All rights reserved. No part of this publication may be reproduced, stored in a
retrieval system, or transmitted in any form, or by any means, electronic,
mechanical, photocopying, recording or otherwise, without the prior
permission of the publishers and copyright holders.

British Library Cataloging in Publication Data

Mountford, Frances
    Commoner's Cottage: Story of a Cottage through the Ages
    I. Title
    942·21

            ISBN 0-7509-0118-7 (hardback)
            ISBN 0-7509-0987-0 (paperback)

Colour separation by Yeo Graphics Reproduction Limited.
Printed in Hong Kong by
Midas Printing Limited.

ACKNOWLEDGEMENTS

My grateful thanks for help and information go to:

Mr. D. C. Christopherson, Mr. and the late Mrs. A. Clark, Mr. D. K. Coles,
Mr. R. Harding, Mrs. M. Hand, Mrs. G. Harmar, Mrs. L. K. Hoad,
Margaret Kohler, Misses D. and E. Mercer, Mr. R. A. Morphett,
Mrs. F. K. Philpott, Mr. R. F. Philpott, Major A. Stephens,
Mr. Bill Smith, Mr. J. E. N. Walker, Mr. M. F. Worsfold,

and special thanks to Mrs. Vivian Ettlinger for reading
the manuscript and for her comments.

Acknowledgements to Boosey and Hawkes Music Publishers Ltd. for
permission to use a verse of "Bless this House", by Helen Taylor, copyright 1932.

A very special thank you to my husband, Alan, for his abiding interest
and encouragement.

Bless this house, O Lord we pray
Make it safe by night and day;
Bless these walls, so firm and stout,
Keeping want and trouble out,

Bless the roof and chimneys tall,
Let thy peace lie over all;
Bless this door that it may prove
Ever open to joy and love

Helen Taylor.

I sing of Brooks, of Blossomes, Birds and Bowers,
Of April, May, of June and July ~ Flowers ~.
I sing of May-poles, Hock-carts, Wassails, Wakes
Of Bride-grooms, Brides, and of their Bridall-cakes;
I write of Youth, of Love, and have Accesse
By these to sing of cleanly-Wantonnesse .....
I sing of Dewes, of Raines, and piece by piece
Of Balm, of Oyle, of Spice, and Amber-Greece ..
I sing of times trans~shifting; and I write
How roses first came Red and Lillies White ....
I write of Groves, of Twilights, and I sing
The Court of Mab, and of the Fairie~King ..
I write of Hell; I sing (and ever shall)
Of Heaven, and hope to have it after all.

Robert Herrick (1591-1674)

F.MOUNTFORD. '80.

In the 21ˢᵀ YEAR of the REIGN of ELIZABETH I
in the COUNTY of SURREY, ENGLAND

JOHN SYMONS, age 23, married WYNIFRETH CHASEMORE, age 29.
on St. Valentine's Day, a propitious date for lovers as it was
traditionally the day on which the birds chose their mates.

1579

14 February   John Symon so Wyniful Chasmour married

Dorking Registers.

They were both from the Manor of Dorking,
where they lived and worked together
afterwards for the rest of their lives.

John and Wynifreth Symons had four children
all baptised at St. Martin's Church, Dorking.

ALICE   baptised 2nd April 1581
AGNES   baptised 21st April 1583
JOHN   baptised 1585, buried 1586
THOMAS   baptised 19th July 1590

At this time babies were breast fed until they had cut four or
more teeth. Afterwards a bottle made from a cow's horn might have
been used. A mother or wet nurse sometimes smeared her
nipples with bitter wormwood in order to discourage the child.

It was believed that an infant could imbibe vices along with
the milk and that children possessed "phlegmatic" stomachs, which
meant that moist and cool foods were best for them, and they
needed nine hours of sleep.

The husbandman all day goeth to plough
And when he comes home he serveth his sow,
He moileth and toileth all the long year
How can he be merry and make good cheer?

from an old rhyme

At this time there was great enthusiasm all over England for building new houses.

JOHN SYMONS probably lived in an old hovel with the fire in the centre of the main room. He very likely worked on the land for a yeoman, or he hired himself out on a casual basis, being a husbandman, with a piece of land on which to grow his own provisions. He would have kept a few animals, which would have been grazed on the common, while WYNIFRETH and his daughters reared poultry.

When his son THOMAS was about a year old JOHN SYMONS took the first step towards acquiring his own house. He applied to the Court Baron in Dorking for a piece of common land. This was probably situated quite close to the hovel in which he was then living.

His request was granted. The clerk wrote in the Rolls:
"John Symonde holds by copy dated 6th day of October 1592 one rood of land out of the Waste......."

· JOHN SYMONS of the HOLMWOOD ·

Regular meetings of the **COURT BARON** and the **COURT LEET** were held within the Manor to deal with the customs and usages. The proceedings of the court were inscribed in the Rolls. Latin was used until 1733 except for the Commonwealth period when they were written in English.

The **COURT BARON** dealt mostly with property, particularly COPYHOLD PROPERTY, which had existed as such since about the middle of the 13th century, (the time when villeins started to become free men), until about 1926. Villeins became copyholders when they obtained written evidence of their right to their holding. When they left it they surrendered the property back to the Lord of the Manor who granted admission to the new tenant. Thus COPYHOLD was so called because the tenant held a copy of his admittance as it was inscribed in the Court Rolls.

The COPYHOLDER could sub-let the property. He was expected to attend the court and make a payment on admission of the new tenant. In the early days the COPYHOLDER was liable to work for a certain number of days a year for the lord. When the copyholder died a heriot of the best beast that he owned was due to the lord, but this became commuted to a cash payment.   The HEIRS of the copyholder were also admitted to the property at a meeting of the Court Baron.

In Surrey the system of BOROUGH ENGLISH prevailed where the property passed to the youngest son, with daughters as co-heirs, as opposed to PRIMOGENITURE where it passed to the eldest son, or "GAVEL-KIND" where it was split between the children.

The **COURT LEET** dealt with misdemeanours. In 1589 JOHN SYMONS was fined three-shillings and four pence for erecting fences on Betchett Green, which was a part of Holmwood Common.

"John Symons incrochia vit supra vast duos apud Bechworth Grene cum sepibus suis......"

THE LORD OF THE MANOR

The Dukes of Norfolk-Earls of Arundel were the lords of the Dorking manor. They were descendants of the family of Warren who were the first of the monarch's subjects to be in possession of the manor from a very early period. They were granted the manor in about 1089.

By the late 1500's the lord of the manor and his tenants' allegiance to him did not affect the day to day lives of the people, but he was an established tradition and a part of the order of their existence. Once upon a time he had demanded that his villeins work only for him upon the manor, but now all his tenants were free men, and had been so for over a century. Still he was the lord, and from the tenants living within the manor he could claim certain rights and dues.

At the time that John Symons applied for his land and cottage the manor was actually in the possession of about four people. The descent of the manor is difficult to trace clearly. Several Dukes met with violent death in the Tower of London. In 1572, by an Act of Parliament, the titles were restored to Philip, Earl of Arundel after his father was beheaded. Philip himself was incarcerated and died there in 1595, but his son Thomas was later restored to all titles.

Besides the Dukes of Norfolk/Earls of Arundel, the descent of the manor included the families of Mowbray, FitzAlan and Beauchamp-Lord Abergavenny.

SOLA VIRTUS INVICTA

8

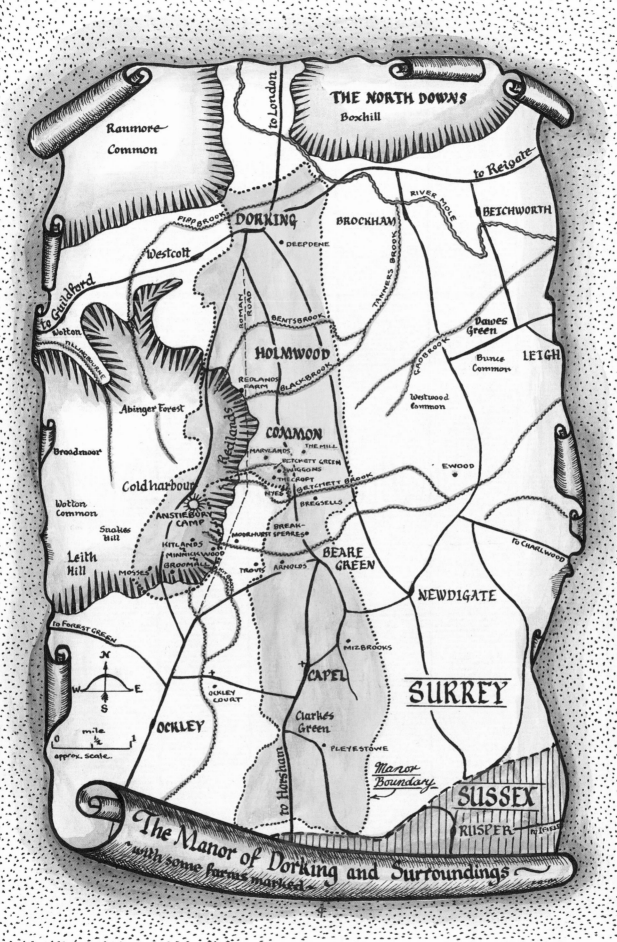

The Manor of Dorking and Surroundings with some farms marked

The **COMMON** was owned by the LORD of the MANOR.

The tenants were limited, or stinted to a certain number of cattle or sheep that they were permitted to turn out onto the common.

The number of animals that a tenant had the right to turn on the common was estimated by those animals "levant and couchant", (i.e. rising up and lying down, or were there day and night), on the tenant's own land during the winter when the grass on the common was not growing.

SOME RIGHTS OF COMMON

pasture
HERBAGE

tree loppings, gorse, underwood
ESTOVERS

turf, peat
TURBARY

beech mast, acorns
PANNAGE

fish
PISCARY

sand, gravel, stone, minerals
COMMON IN THE SOIL

There were two forms of COMMON of PASTURE:

✳ COMMON APPENDANT. The origin was probably not Manorial. It was the right of freehold tenants to depasture their commonable cattle. Commonable cattle were beasts of the plough (horses or oxen) and animals which manure the land (cows and sheep). As tilling the land was desirable, a tenant needed these animals to carry it out, and grazing for them.

✳ COMMON APPURTENANT. This applied where the occupiers of a specific house had been given a grant, or could prove long use beforehand, and so had the right to use the common. Swine, goats, donkeys and geese were not commonable creatures, but occasionally the right to graze these might be a common appurtenant.

10

THE LAND · John's rood of land was on the Green, where he had previously erected the fences for which he had been fined.

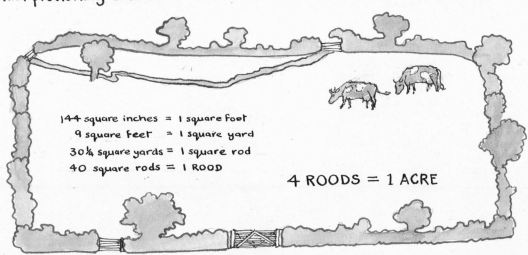

144 square inches = 1 square foot
9 square feet = 1 square yard
30¼ square yards = 1 square rod
40 square rods = 1 ROOD

4 ROODS = 1 ACRE

The Green was a part of Holmwood Common, in the form of an arm of it which extended towards the tree covered hills. Except for that side of the Green which joined the open common it was surrounded by enclosed fields. It was a flatish area of about three acres, with banks and ditches dividing it from the fields. On the north and south boundaries streams of clear water purled down from the hills, their banks fringed with bluebells, wild garlic, dog's mercury and ferns.

The Green was a meeting point for several tracks. It was as if it had been, in the long forgotten days, part of a great web of paths and greens which had netted the country. The long dead people had created them, hewing and burning forest to make clearings on which to live and to herd their animals.

The main track from this Green ran in a north-south direction. Northwards it ran, with hardly a curve, over the stream and directly to Dorking town. Southwards it crossed the other stream and went towards Capel village. Another path led past Nyes farm, and yet another crossed the old Devil's Stoney Street, properly called the Roman Stane Street. This path continued up a steep hill to ancient Anstiebury Camp and to the high woodlands, heathlands and commons that stretched to Guildford, and beyond.

Despite so many paths converging there, people travelling between Dorking and Horsham probably did not cross the Green very often in these days. Now that enclosed fields surrounded most of it they would tend to make their way across the open common a quarter of a mile or so to the east, although the common was swampy and heavy going.

The Hearth Room in the Old House

The Elizabethan age was a time of GREAT REBUILDING. Splendid manor houses were built as well as more modest dwellings. England was peaceful and the country as a whole was wealthy.

by Robert Herrick 1591 – 1674

So Good-luck came, and on my roofe did light
Like noyse-less Snow, or as the dew of night;
Not all at once, but gently, as the trees
Are, by the Sun-beams, tickel'd by degrees.

"He that builds a fair house upon an ill seat committeth himself to prison." Francis Bacon

NURSERY RHYME
(believed to owe its origin to a chaldee hymn).

This is the farmer who sowed the corn,
That kept the cock that crowed in the morn,
That waked the priest all shaven and shorn,
That married the man all tattered and torn,
That kissed the maiden all forlorn,
That milked the cow with the crumpled horn,
That tossed the dog, that worried the cat,
That killed the rat, that ate the malt
That lay in the HOUSE THAT JACK BUILT

Queen Elizabeth decreed in 1589 that every new house should be constructed within four acres of ground. This was to prevent the spread of fire and disease and to conserve timber. The decree went largely unheeded throughout the country.

Elizabethans believed that:
the south wind doth corrupt and make for evil vapours."
All the same many houses were built facing southwards.

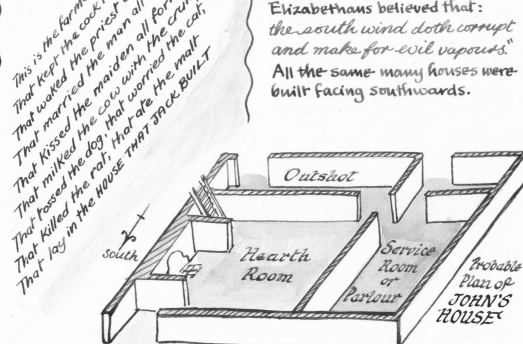

south

Outshot

Hearth Room

Service Room or Parlour

Probable Plan of JOHN'S HOUSE

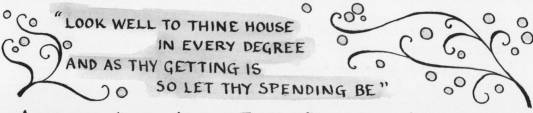

"LOOK WELL TO THINE HOUSE
          IN EVERY DEGREE
AND AS THY GETTING IS
          SO LET THY SPENDING BE"

A verse carved upon a beam at Trouts, a farm built in the nearby manor of Ockley in 1500 and added to in 1581

"You must eat within your tether"
an old saying

Coins of Queen Elizabeth I

Sovereign	30s or	£1.50p
Ryal	15s or	75p
Angel	10s or	50p
Half Angel	5s or	25p
Quarter Angel	2s6d or	12½p
Pound	20s or	£1.00
Half Pound	10s or	50p
Crown	5s or	25p
Half Crown	2s6d or	12½p
Shilling	1s or	5p
Sixpence	6d or	2½p
Groat	4⅙d	
Half Groat	2¼d	
Threepence	3d	
Threehalfpence	1½d	
Penny	1d	
Threefarthings	¾d	
Halfpenny	½d	
Farthing	¼d	

reverse side — Gold Angel

Silver Crown

The Queen herself was very thrifty

"The Money of England was abafed and falfified for a long time, till Queen Elizabeth in the year 1560, to Her great praife, called in all such Money; since which time, no bafe Money hath been coyned in England, but onely of pure Gold and Silver, called Sterling Money; onely of latter times, in relation to the neceffity of the Poor, and exchange of great Money, a Small piece of Brafs, called a Farthing, or Fourth part of a Penny, hath been permitted to be Coyned, but no man enforced to receive them in pay for Rent or Debt ...."

from THE PRESENT STATE OF ENGLAND, by Edward Chamberlayne. 1676

14

In the winter of 1592 or 1593 oaks for the new house were felled. The oaks would have been between 40 and 100 years old, growing straight and tall through coppiced hazel. While the wood was still green it was easier to saw and to shape with an adye. When allowed to weather for a year or more oak becomes so hard and tough it quickly dulls an axe.

AN ADZE

The trees would require only a little squaring off to neaten them up and to make them into the main load-bearing beams of the house. For the smaller beams some trunks would be riven by hammering wedges into them until they split lengthways.

Each tree trunk, as it was riven and shaped, was made for its allotted place in the plan of the house. The greatest timbers were for the cills which would lie flat upon the ground and upon which the entire house would rest. Next in size were the main vertical posts. Then there were long and thick tie beams, arch braces for the corners and short and more slender studs. The floor boards, being broad and flat had to be sawn over a pit, with one man in the pit itself, sawdust falling all over him, and one man at the other end of the saw, standing above. The floor boards, however, were usually made of softer wood than oak. Many of them measured eighteen inches wide.

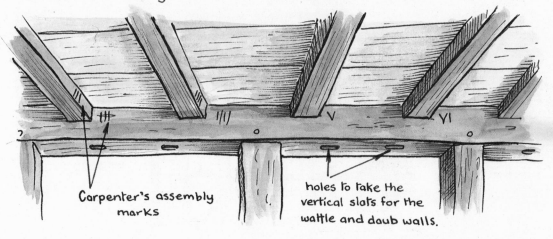

Carpenter's assembly marks

holes to take the vertical slats for the wattle and daub walls.

The Ceiling Beam dividing the Hearth Room from the East Room.

Oxen hauled the ready-shaped timbers to John Symons' patch of land on the Green. As the ground round about was liable to be wet and heavy the carpenter probably waited for a sharp frost to make the hauling easier.

The timbers would have been laid out in rough order upon the ground with several men setting about the task of erecting the framework of the house. Then the air would have been loud with the sound of the heart of oak pegs being hammered into the holes of the mortice and tenon joints, with the rattle and creaking of the pulley lifting the heavy timbers, and the chopping and sawing of the carpenter as he made a little more leeway in a joint, or took an inch or two off the end of a beam.

As the oak dried out it would move and shrink. In years to come it would harden like iron and after that it would settle and shift hardly at all.

The framework of the house stood gaunt: an angular wooden skeleton, awaiting the arrival of tiles, bricks, and wattle and daub for the walls.

Despite the opinions of some people that south facing houses were susceptible to plague-bearing winds, John Symons' house faced southwards so that the sunlight could shine into the mullioned windows and warm the rooms, especially in winter time when the sun rode low across the sky and its rays could penetrate to the furthest wall of the hearth room.

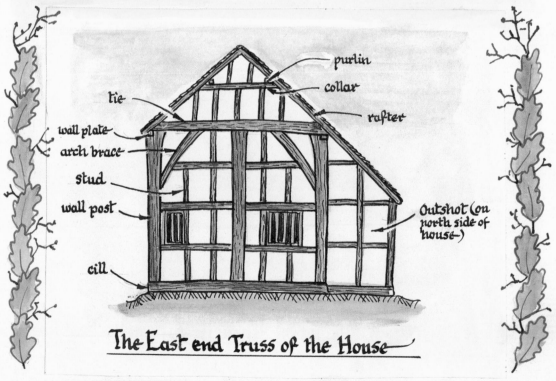

The East end Truss of the House

Just as the area grew fine oak trees, so the Wealden clay was perfect for making bricks.

Despite an abundance of local clay, bricks were expensive, for it was slow and laborious work to make them.

The clay had to be dug from the ground in autumn and left in heaps to temper over the winter. Not until the end of March did brick-making begin, but then, if the weather was wet the bricks would not dry out and could not be fired until fine weather came again.

Only rich people could afford to have the whole of the infilling between the timber framework built up with bricks. Husbandmen of John's status had to settle for wattle and daub for most walls.

Bricks were a necessity around the fireplace for the smoke bay.

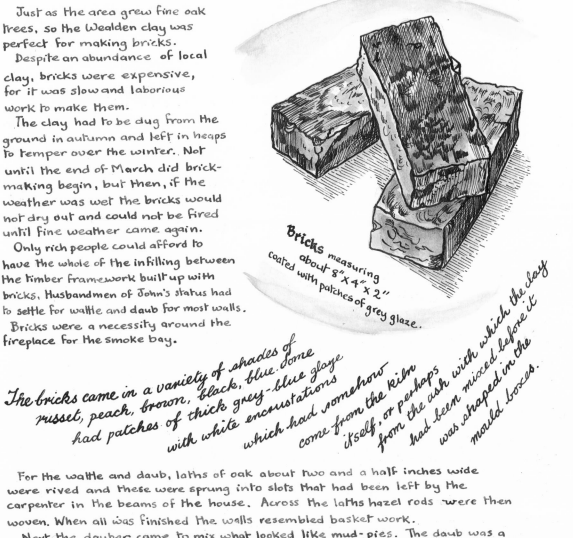

Bricks measuring about 8" x 4" x 2" coated with patches of grey glaze.

The bricks came in a variety of shades of russet, peach, brown, black, blue. Some had patches of thick grey-blue glaze with white encrustations which had somehow come from the kiln itself, or perhaps from the ash with which the clay had been mixed before it was shaped in the mould boxes.

For the wattle and daub, laths of oak about two and a half inches wide were rived and these were sprung into slots that had been left by the carpenter in the beams of the house. Across the laths hazel rods were then woven. When all was finished the walls resembled basket work.

Next the dauber came to mix what looked like mud-pies. The daub was a mixture of clay, cow dung, lime, chaff and sheep's wool. When it was of the correct consistency he expertly slapped it across the oak laths and hazel rods so that it lay smooth. The sheep's wool prevented the daub cracking up as it dried.

While the daub was still wet the dauber roughened the surface with a bunch of birch twigs, so that the lime plaster, which would be thinly applied over the top, would easily adhere to it.

Wattle and Daub ~

> *"John Symons holdeth a cottage sett upon the Lords Waste at Betchett Greene containing 1R. to him granted — Court 20 May Anno 36 Eliz iiijd*

By now John had made other applications to the Court Baron and he appears to have held 4 roods (1acre) of land at Betchett Green.

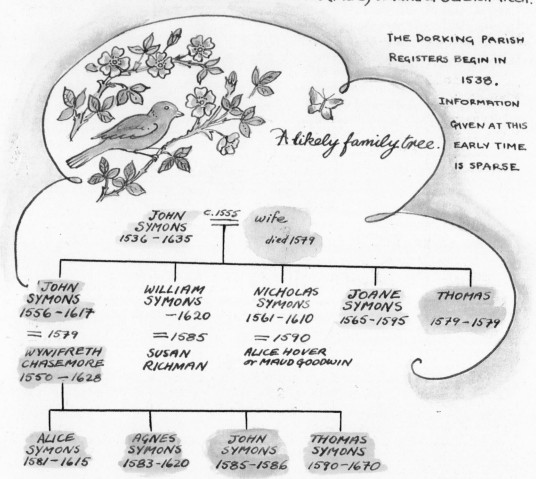

THE DORKING PARISH REGISTERS BEGIN IN 1538. INFORMATION GIVEN AT THIS EARLY TIME IS SPARSE

A likely family tree.

JOHN SYMONS 1536 - 1635   c.1555   wife died 1579

JOHN SYMONS 1556 - 1617 = 1579 WYNIFRETH CHASEMORE 1550 — 1628

WILLIAM SYMONS — 1620 = 1585 SUSAN RICHMAN

NICHOLAS SYMONS 1561 - 1610 = 1590 ALICE HOVER or MAUD GOODWIN

JOANE SYMONS 1565 - 1595

THOMAS 1579 - 1579

ALICE SYMONS 1581 - 1615

AGNES SYMONS 1583 - 1620

JOHN SYMONS 1585 - 1586

THOMAS SYMONS 1590 - 1670

JOHN SYMONS was age 37, his wife WYNIFRETH age 43, daughter ALICE age 12, AGNES age 10, and son THOMAS age 3, when they moved into the new house. They may have been accompanied by John's sister JOANE, age 28, and by his father JOHN, age 57. (John's mother had died in 1579, the same year as his baby brother Thomas died, and the same year, too, that John married Wynifreth. Perhaps, after her marriage, Wynifreth took charge of the whole Symons family, as Joane would have been only thirteen years old then).

MOVING IN

Into the new house went all the family's stored food, their tools and implements and their few pieces of furniture.

The week's baking would have been bundled up and the smoked and salted meat and fish, although, had they moved in spring, the greater part of this would already have been eaten over winter.

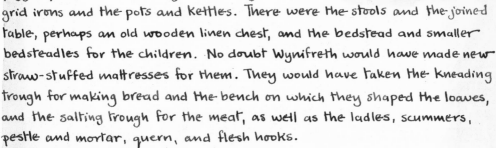

Then there were the water carriers, and piggin pails, the fire tongs and hangers, the grid irons and the pots and kettles. There were the stools and the joined table, perhaps an old wooden linen chest, and the bedstead and smaller bedsteadles for the children. No doubt Wynifreth would have made new straw-stuffed mattresses for them. They would have taken the kneading trough for making bread and the bench on which they shaped the loaves, and the salting trough for the meat, as well as the ladles, scummers, pestle and mortar, quern, and flesh hooks.

THE SMOKE BAY

In the new house the fire was no longer in the centre of the room, but set to one side so that the smoke rose within its own narrow bay where meat and fish were hung high up for smoking. At this time the house still had no chimney. The smoke went out through a hole in the roof.

Chimneys were built mainly in gentlemens' large residences.

Some people did not approve of smoke bays because they took more smoke out of the room. They believed that breathing in smoke kept away colds and illness.

The new house still smelled like the out-of-doors, for it did not reek with the smoke and sweat of centuries like the hovel they had left. The daub was barely dried out, and the earthen floor, beneath a clean layer of glistening rushes, was still damp.

There was no scent in it yet of woodsmoke or stored apples, no smells of new-baked bread or salted meat had permeated the wooden beams, no pigs or fowls ran in and out to add their own distinctive odours.

Perhaps they held a feast to celebrate moving in, with:

roast beef • mutton • roasted capons • rabbit pie • brawn • shallots • cheeses • ham • gingerbread • cabbage • marchpane • tansie pudding • fruit pies • sugar sops • junket • oranges • beer • home-made wine • oat cakes

" WINE MAKES OLD WIVES WENCHES "   "AS DRUNK AS A MOUSE "

" The situation of our region, lying near unto the north, doth cause the heat of our stomacks to be of somewhat greater force: therefore our bodies do crave a little more ample nourishment than the inhabitants of hotter regions are accustomed withal, whose digestive force is not altogether so vehement, because their internal heat is not so strong as ours, which is kept in by the coldness of the air that from time to time (especially in winter) doth environ our bodies. It is no marvel therefore that our tables are oftentimes more plentifully garnished than other nations ......"

William Harrison. Description of England 1587.

The staple diet for ordinary people was beef, bread and beer.

Queen Elizabeth instructed her people to eat fish on Fridays instead of meat. This was to encourage the fishing industry in the coastal towns.

Cook shops in towns sold such things as mackerel, hot sheeps' feet, oysters, ribs of beef, meat pies, brawn, etc.

People ate with their fingers. Large dishes were placed in the centre of the table and they served themselves onto wooden trenchers.

They used a knife for meat and bread, and a spoon for soup and dessert, but there were no forks.

Water was not considered wholesome to drink. Most people drank beer, occasionally they would drink cider or home-made wine.

It was usually the womenfolk who malted the barley, done by soaking it for four days, then alternately piling it up and spreading it until it had sprouted (after about ten days), then drying it and crushing it in a mortar. This was malt.

ALE: was made from fermented malt before hops were grown in England.

BEER: Hops were increasingly grown in England during Elizabeth's reign and beer was made from malt and hops, fermented with yeast.

Eight hundred pints of beer per person per year were drunk.

To Make a Mince Pie

Cut the best of the flesh from a leg of mutton and parboil it well. Add 3lb of best mutton suet and shred it small. Season with pepper, salt, cloves and mace. Add currants, great raisins, prunes, a few sliced dates and sliced orange-pills. Mix all together, put in coffins and bake. When served up, open the lids and strew sugar on top of the meat and lid.

As directed by GERVASE MARKHAM.

WOMEN'S WORK

On Mondays and Thursdays, the Dorking market days, the family went to town to buy and to sell, and again they walked in on Sundays to attend church.

The family would have been almost self-supporting, with the women folk working very hard.

The women saw to the dairy produce or "white meat." They probably owned one or two cows, and from their milk would make some butter or cheese. Hard cheese, which kept well, was made from skimmed milk, while a small amount of soft cheese from whole milk would have been made.

At Martinmas, in November, animals were killed before they grew thin on the diminishing grass, and before they needed extra fodder. This was a busy time for the women when they were cutting up meat, pickling pieces of it in brine in the salting trough, or rubbing in bay salt and salt-petre to preserve it.

Afterwards it was hung above the fire in the smoke bay to catch the smoke.

The smoke of burning oak logs produced meat of better flavour than the smoke of other woods.

Every week there was a batch of loaves to be baked. Nowadays they did not often do the querning by hand but relied upon the mills at Capel or Dorking to grind their corn. The quern they now used mostly for grinding malt for beer, or for making bean flour, while a separate little quern was for mustard seed.

The women never had an idle moment, for besides the annual work in the fields with which they helped: the hay-making, harvesting, stone-picking, clod-breaking, weeding, and other like tasks, they malted the barley for beer, made rush lights, carried water, cultivated the garden, watched the animals on the common, tended the poultry, cured skins, did some weaving, made pies and cakes, boiled meats and vegetables, attended to the children, and, to fill in every spare moment, carried with them a spindle for spinning wool or flax.

MEN'S WORK

It is likely that the menfolk of the family would have hired themselves out for work locally from time to time. For general farm work they were able to earn about 7d a day each.

At home they would cultivate the ground which had been enclosed with the house, planting an orchard, growing some corn and perhaps some flax. The immediate tasks at the new house would have been planting a hedge to prevent other peoples' animals from straying inside, digging drainage ditches, making shelters for cattle and new coops for poultry. They would need a woodshed so that kindling and dead wood brought in from the common, as well as dried cattle dung, could be kept dry, for the fire was essential for their well-being. In bad weather they mended tools, made and repaired harness, made baskets, and turned their hands to almost any other task that presented itself.

From the SURREY MUSTERS 1596
(Selected Names).

DORKING.
Thomas Heybette
William Symon
Robert Symon } struck out
Thomas Hooker }
John Palmer
John Symon — struck out
William Hooker
William Symon — struck out

From the SURREY MUSTERS 1583/4
(Selected Names)

DORKING
William Chasemore · billman
William Symons · billman

HOMEWOOD
Thomas Boxall · billman
Thomas Symons · billman
William Symons · billman
Robert Peter · billman
William Wonham · archer

CAPEL
William Chasemore · billman
John Chasemore, Snr. billman
Robert Younge · billman
Henry Swan · billman

OCKLEY
John Stere · pikeman
John Chasemore · billman
Ralphe Baxe · archer
Richard Chasemore · archer

16th century wall painting preserved from a house in Dorking.

CROPS and WEATHER

1591 A year of drought.
1592 A severe winter followed by a dry year.
1593 Likely to have been a poor harvest as wheat prices rose the following year.
1594 Rain fell almost incessantly from early May to July 25th with a consequently poor harvest.
1595 Another poor harvest
1596 Again a poor harvest. Famine in Europe.
1597 A famine year. Wheat at 92s. a quarter.
1598 A better year. The price of wheat dropped.
1599 A good harvest year.

23

WYNIFRETH and THOMAS

Border design adapted from a 16th century wall painting in a house in Dorking High Street. Fragments of the painting are preserved in Dyas hardware shop.

On 9th SEPTEMBER 1595   JOANE SYMONS was buried at ST. MARTIN'S, DORKING.

She would have been 30 years old.
It is not known how or why she died.

Almost everyone caught SMALLPOX at sometime during their lives with varying degrees of severity.

After catching the virus people are contagious for about three weeks.

The disease begins like influenza with a high temperature, headache, sickness and pain and aching in the muscles

On the fourth day a rash appears, with spots particularly on the head and limbs. The spots become filled with a fluid which is clear at first but then turns to yellow pus.

The spots burst and the yellow matter runs out over the body and smells with a foul odour. There are sometimes pustules in the mouth and throat too.

If the afflicted person survives, the pustules heal over after about three weeks leaving the skin pitted with pock marks. It was believed that if a piece of red cloth was hung up against the window during the illness the pock marks would be lessened.

Sufferers of smallpox should stay in bed with a fluid diet, but infections of the skin and mouth, pleurisy and deafness sometimes result.

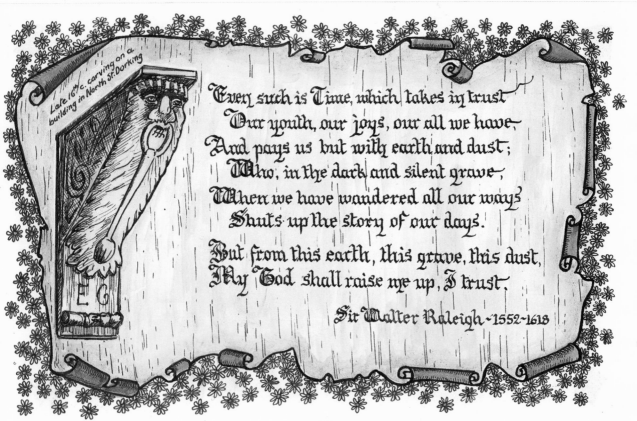

Late 16th c. carving on a building in North St. Dorking

E G

Every such is Time, which takes in trust
Our youth, our joys, our all we have,
And pays us but with earth and dust;
Who, in the dark and silent grave,
When we have wandered all our ways
Shuts up the story of our days.

But from this earth, this grave, this dust,
My God shall raise me up, I trust.

Sir Walter Raleigh ~ 1552-1618

A NEW CENTURY

On Thursday 24ᵗʰ March 1603
Queen Elizabeth ~ Good Queen Bess ~ died ⌒

"There was no hope of her recovery, because she refused all remedies. On Wednesday, the 23rd of March, she grew speechless. That afternoon, by signs she called for her Council: and by putting her hand to her head, when the King of Scots was named to succeed her, they all knew he was the man she desired should reign after her. About six at night, she made signs for the Archbishop, and her chaplains to come to her; at which time, I went in with them, and sat upon my knees full of tears to see that heavy sight. Her Majesty lay upon her back, with one hand in the bed and the other without."

"----- Between one and two of the clock on Thursday morning, he that I left in the cofferer's chamber, brought me word that the Queen was dead."

Memoirs of Sir Robert Carey

Rosemary for remembrance

In 1603 in Dorking there were over a hundred deaths caused by THE PLAGUE. Often whole families caught it and all died. To save infection by carrying the corpses to the churchyard many were buried nearby in fields or gardens.

There were regular occurrences of the disease, with some years worse than others.

1608 · A Wedding between ALICE SYMONS and JOHN HOOKER,

at St. Martin's Church, Dorking, 2nd April 1608

Alice was 27 years old, and the first person to be married from the new house.

It was the custom to give gloves at weddings —

For poorer people, invited guests left presents on a table in the church —

All pins from the bride's garland or dress had to be thrown away, or else the marriage would be unhappy —

The bride wore several garters and there was an undignified scramble for them by the young men after the ceremony. They wore them on their hats and jackets at the feast

The "Bridale" or wedding feast was so called because brides of the lower classes sometimes sold ale to their friends on the wedding day for whatever the friends would give.

27

Squatters

The custom prevailed that if a man went onto the Common or wasteland and could manage to erect some sort of dwelling which had a roof during the course of one night, and which had a fire burning in the hearth by morning, then he was entitled to stay and call the primitive building his home. He did not need permission from the legitimate landholder.

Thus on a cloudless night, with a bright moon to give light to work by, such hovels would be thrown up, made of posts, branches, turves, heather, gorse and mud, with a hearth of stones.

Local, respectable, people complained about such squatters taking pieces of their Common and depriving them of grazing but there was little they could do about it. They saw the newcomers as shifty and untrustworthy people who seemed to live on nothing for they had no proper work. The squatters existed as best as they could, taking advantage of what the Common had to offer in the way of peckings for a few fowl, fuel for their fires, and heather and birch for making brooms to sell. Many stole and poached and lived out their poor lives as best as they could.

In the early seventeenth century squatters settled on wasteland in many parts of England. The squatter families on the Holmwood Common never numbered more than about twenty-five on a waste of nearly eight hundred acres.

JAMES I – age 36 in 1603 – about 5 million people in England.

His accession marked the beginning of a long struggle for power between King and Parliament.

James and his successors believed that a king should be able to override the wishes of Parliament.

Parliament felt that the King must govern according to the policy laid down by Parliament.

James VI of Scotland, son of Mary, Queen of Scots, and Lord Darnley.

1603-1625

James I of England.

James was a lazy and extravagant king but his reign was a time of peace and tolerance.

Only the king could summon, adjourn or dissolve Parliament, but he did not have sufficient wealth to run the country indefinitely without recourse to Parliament. ~ James's difficulties were made greater because of the religious differences between his people.

1605

A group of Roman Catholics plotted to blow up Parliament on a day when they knew the king would be present. Twenty barrels of gunpowder were discovered, and one of the conspirators, Guy Fawkes, was captured in a cellar beneath the House of Lords. The other conspirators were caught and were executed.

1609

The first English colony settled on the mainland of North America in Virginia, which had been discovered in 1576.

1611

James authorised a new translation of the Bible. Fifty-four translators were engaged to work on it. This popular Authorised Version was still in use more than three and a half centuries later.

1620

A party of English Puritans, called The Pilgrim Fathers, sailed across the Atlantic in The "Mayflower" and settled north of Virginia in what became New England.

𝔇eath was a frequent occurrence in most families.

Poor people were not usually buried in coffins, nor were their graves marked.
People threw evergreens, such as bay, rosemary or yew into the graves as a sign of the soul's immortality. Garlands of flowers were placed on the grave, too, and hung in the church, especially if the dead person were a young unmarried woman.

It was the custom to wail and howl at funerals.
There would be a feast after the funeral, with guests contributing if the people were poor.

1613 The couple who had been married only five years before, JOHN and ALICE (née SYMONS) HOOKER both died. JOHN HOOKER was buried on 1st February and ALICE a few days later. They left two little children: JOHN and AGNES.

1614 It was a very cruel winter with deep snow which lay for two whole months from January 16th onwards. Fodder for the animals was in very short supply.

1615 After the New Year began, (at this time the New Year started on March 25th), there had at last been a thaw, but some more snow followed and then a frost so that planting was late. On May Day snow flakes fluttered down. There followed two months of drought in summer.
The following January little AGNES HOOKER, the grandchild of JOHN and WYNIFRETH SYMONS, died.

1616 Another dry summer. Wheat was 40s. 8d per quarter, which was an average price for these years.

1617 JOHN SYMONS of Betchett Green died, age 61 years, and was buried at St. Martin's, Dorking, on 15th April. He was survived by his widow WYNIFRETH daughter AGNES and son THOMAS. The JOHN SYMONS who was probably his father was still alive too.
At this time THOMAS took over the Copyhold.

CALENDAR

MARCH 25TH – LADY DAY This marked the beginning of the New Year on the Calendar. Lady Day commemorates the Annunciation of the Virgin Mary. It marks one of the Quarter Days of England when rents become due.

FOURTH SUNDAY IN LENT – MOTHERING SUNDAY. Folk visited their parents taking them nosegays. Simnel cake was eaten.

SUNDAY BEFORE EASTER – PALM SUNDAY. The people carried willow, yew or box into church in memory of Christ's triumphal entry into Jerusalem.

THURSDAY BEFORE EASTER – MAUNDY THURSDAY. There was a custom of shaving and cutting hair on this day, and alms giving to the poor.

GOOD FRIDAY People attended church, ate hot cross buns, gave each other "pace-eggs" which were hard boiled eggs with their shells dyed various colours.

EASTER SUNDAY (falling on a Sunday between 22nd March and 25th April according to the moon). Fasting over Lent came to an end.

EASTER MONDAY. Soul cakes were made and given to the poor. Sports and games were played, such as stool-ball and barley-brake.

SECOND MONDAY AND TUESDAY AFTER EASTER – HOCKTIDE. Money was collected for charitable purposes by men binding with cords any women they met and receiving payment for release. Women bound the men on the next day.

MAY 1ST – MAY DAY The great rural festival of the year, with the Maypole erected in towns and villages, morris dances, pageants.

"The Maypole is up,
    Now give me the cup
        I'll drink to the garlands around it,
            But first unto those
                Whose hands did compose
                    The glory of flowers that crown'd it"

FIFTH SUNDAY AFTER EASTER — ROGATION SUNDAY. The clergy went out into the fields to bless the crops.

MONDAY, TUESDAY and WEDNESDAY before ASCENSION DAY — ROGATION DAYS In many parishes the boundaries were walked and the elders of the parish whipped boys with willow wands at certain points so that they would not forget the boundary.

SEVENTH SUNDAY AFTER EASTER — WHITSUNTIDE, followed by WHITSUNTIDE WEEK A time of feasting and country dancing.

JUNE 23RD — MIDSUMMER EVE Bonfires at midnight.

JUNE 24TH — ST. JOHN'S DAY or MIDSUMMER DAY One of the quarter days of England when rents are due.

JULY 15TH — ST. SWITHIN'S DAY An old superstition is that if rain falls on St. Swithin's Day it will rain for forty days.

AUGUST 1ST — LAMMAS Fences were removed from common land which had been cultivated during summer, and livestock was permitted to graze over it until it was re-seeded again. An old quarter day.

HARVEST HOME Celebrations at the end of harvest, with the last patch of the last field cut ceremoniously and this corn made into a sheaf decorated with ribbons, and a procession of the labourers and their wives following the last load. There would be a feast at the master's house, with singing and dancing to follow.

SEPTEMBER 29TH — MICHAELMAS DAY One of the quarter days in England. The time when the landlord held a feast for all his tenants after his rents were collected. Michaelmas dinner was very often goose. Michaelmas was the termination date for men and women who had been hired as labourers and servants and fairs the year before.

OCTOBER – Fairs were held in the market towns and villages when animals and produce were sold, and labourers and servants hired.

OCTOBER 31ST – ALL HALLOW EVEN or HALLOWE'EN. The night when witches are abroad and the country folk took precautions to safeguard themselves and their animals; and the night when ghosts appear.

NOVEMBER 1ST and 2ND – ALL SAINTS and ALL SOULS Prayers for the dead. Children and adults went begging for soul-cakes and other gifts.

NOVEMBER 11TH – MARTINMAS Once a quarter day in England. A feast day.

ADVENT SUNDAY The Christian year commences four weeks preceeding Christmas.

DECEMBER 13TH – ST. LUCY'S DAY The shortest day (before the new calendar was introduced)

DECEMBER 24TH – CHRISTMAS EVE. The Yule log, with holly and mistletoe brought indoors.

DECEMBER 25TH – CHRISTMAS DAY. A quarter day and a day of feasting.

– Leather Jack Jug –

by George Gascoigne 1552-77

And when the tenants come to pay
            their quarter's rent
They bring some fowls at Midsummer,
        a dish of fish at Lent
At Christmas a capon, at Michaelmas
            a goose,
And somewhat else at New Year's
    tide for fear their lease fly loose.

JANUARY 1ST Celebrated as the start of the year (although the year date was unchanged), with Wassail bowls of spiced ale, and gifts.

JANUARY 5TH – TWELFTH NIGHT A rustic festival. Wassailing the apple-orchards in some areas.

THE MONDAY AFTER JAN. 6TH (EPIPHANY) – PLOUGH MONDAY. Festive day with a procession, including the decorated plough to mark the return to work after the Christmas festivities.

FEBRUARY 2ND – CANDLEMAS DAY. A church festival to commemorate the purification of the Virgin. Candles consecrated and carried in procession.

FEBRUARY 14TH – ST. VALENTINE'S DAY. The day for meeting one's true love and giving presents.

BETWEEN 2ND FEB. and 8TH MARCH – SHROVE TUESDAY. The day before commencement of Lent. Pancakes eaten; popular day for cockfights and football in the town streets.

ASH WEDNESDAY. (Forty days before Easter Day). The first day of Lent. "Remember, man, that thou art of ashes, and into dust thou wilt revert."

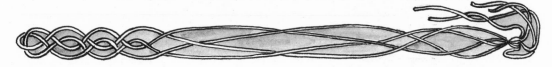

~ A Wood Turner ~

One would imagine that, at 38 years old Agnes Symons would have been a confirmed spinster. Her brother Thomas was 31 years old, but with both his mother and his sister at home he might have felt that to bring in a new bride would make for an unharmonious household.

Perhaps Thomas offered a good dowry to the man who would take his sister off his hands, perhaps Agnes and the woodturner were friends of longstanding, or perhaps the woodturner, a widower since only August 1620, was anxious to acquire another wife and helpmate quickly.

MATHEW COOKE married AGNES SYMONS
at Dorking on 30th April 1621

Agnes's husband would have spent most of his working day at a pole-lathe. On this he could turn green wood staves into such things as ladder rungs, tool handles and stool legs. He would make beakers, bowls and platters, too.

The **POLE LATHE** is one of the oldest devices used for turning wood. The stave to be turned is fixed so that it can revolve between two uprights. A string or leather strap is wound round the stave, one end of the string being fixed to a treadle low down, and the other end connected to a flexible pole fixed by its one end above the lathe.

When the turner presses with his foot on the treadle the string is pulled downwards so that the stave rotates towards him. When he releases the treadle the natural spring in the pole above pulls the string upwards and turns the stave the other way, so that the turner, holding his chisel against the stave can shave it to shape as it rotates.

Buttery Extension with Solar Room above | Hearth Room | Parlour or Service Room

POSSIBLE APPEARANCE AFTER THE EXTENSION WAS BUILT.

It could not have been long after his sister's wedding that Thomas Symons himself took a wife. His bride's name was Ann, but exactly where and when they were married has not been traced.

At about the same time Thomas decided to improve the house, no doubt partly to please Ann. He had the house extended on the western end beyond the smoke bay, to make a buttery with a room above it, and he probably had a staircase built in place of the old stepladder. Almost certainly he had a chimney constructed too. Thomas could not have been poor, but he would not have had glass in his windows, the new ones would have been constructed in the same way as the old with mullion bars and shutters to draw, in bad weather.

Chimneys now were very fashionable and towns were beginning to bristle with them, because they conducted the smoke out of the house and carried it clear of the roof tops much more efficiently than just having a hole in the roof. So common had chimneys become that, for safety's sake, in 1621, an order had been passed saying that they should be built of brick and must be four and a half feet above the roof.

The chimney that Thomas Symons had built on his house was constructed inside the smoke bay, starting wide at the bottom just above the fire and narrowing as it rose within the bay and up to the peak of the roof. Across it inside were fixed iron bars on which meat could be hung for smoking. In the buttery a fireplace was made back to back with the one in the hearth room.

The extension was built in the same way as the first part of the house, with an oak frame-work filled in by wattle and daub pannels.

A Thanksgiving to God

by Robert Herrick

Low is my porch, as is my fate;
    Both void of state;
And yet the threshold of my door
    Is worn by th' poor,
Who thither come, and freely get
    Good words, or meat.
Like as my parlour, so my hall
    And kitchen's small;
A little buttery, and therin
    A little bin,
Which keeps my little loaf of bread
    Unchipt, unflead;
Some brittle sticks of thorn or briar
    Make me a fire,
Close by whose living coal I sit,
    And glow like it.
Lord, I confess too, when I dine,
    The pulse is Thine,
And all those other bits that be
    There placed by Thee;
The worts, the purslain, and the mess
    Of water-cress,
Which of Thy kindness Thou hast sent;
    And my content
Makes those, and my beloved beet,
    To be more-sweet.
'Tis Thou that crown'st my glittering hearth
    With gitless mirth,
And giv'st me wassail bowls to drink,
    Spiced to the brink.
Lord, 'tis Thy plenty-dropping hand
    That soils my land.
And giv'st me, for my bushel sown,
    Twice ten for one;
Thou mak'st my teeming hen to lay
    Her egg each day;
Besides, my healthful ewes to bear
    Me twins each year;
The while the conduits of my kine
    Run cream, for wine:
All these, and better, Thou dost send
    Me, to this end—

That I should render
    for my part,
A thankful heart;
Which, fired with incence,
    I resign,
As wholly Thine;
—But the acceptance,
    that must be,
My Christ, by Thee?

Lord, thou hast given me a cell
    Wherein to dwell;
A little house, whose humble roof
    Is weather proof;
Under the spars of which I lie
    Both soft and dry;
Where Thou my chamber for to ward,
    Hast set a guard
Of harmless thoughts, to watch and keep
    Me, while I sleep.

Design adapted from early 16th century illumination.

Births and Deaths

```
                      THOMAS and ANN
                          SYMONS
   ┌──────────────────────────┼──────────────────────────┐
   THOMAS                 JANE (or JOANE)              JOHN
 SYMONS junior               SYMONS                   SYMONS
christened 6 January 1625  christened 12 October 1628  christened 18 May 1632
                                                    believed to have died a baby
```

King JAMES I died. The people had not regarded him with the affection they had accorded ELIZABETH. CHARLES I came to the throne.

In the same year WYNIFRETH SYMONS died, age 78, buried at St. Martin's, Dorking, on 11th June 1628

In the registers was written:

FRENWYTH SYMONS UXOR JOHN

CHARLES I dissolved Parliament in 1629. For eleven years there was discontent at his methods of raising money and at his attempt to invade Scotland.

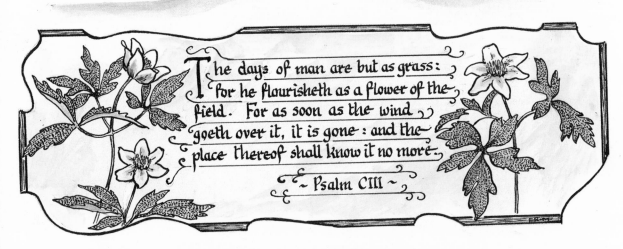

The days of man are but as grass: for he flourisheth as a flower of the field. For as soon as the wind goeth over it, it is gone: and the place thereof shall know it no more.

~ Psalm CIII ~

JOHN SYMONS (who was the probable grand-father of Thomas) was buried at St. Martin's Church, Dorking on 6th December 1635. Usually only the names and dates were inscribed in St. Martin's registers, but, owing to his great age there was written;

JOHN SYMONS AGED 99 YEARS.

A CHILD — He is nature's fresh picture drawn newly in oil, which time and much handling dims and defaces. His soul is yet a white paper unscribbled with observations of the world, wherewith at length it becomes a blurred note-book.

JOHN EARLE - 1628

We are such stuff

As dreams are made on, and our little life

Is rounded with a sleep.

WILLIAM SHAKESPEARE.

1630's

Old John Symons had died at a time when the tenor of life in England was on the verge of changing. There had been several bad harvests and wheat cost more than 56 shillings a quarter.

There were more poor and hungry people in the country than there had been formerly. These put a strain on the Poor Rate money which was paid out by the Overseers of the Poor to those parishioners who were in desperate straights. The Overseers were responsible-minded yeomen who lived within the Manor and who took turns at the job, being guided as to who was deserving of the Poor Rate by the churchwardens and the justices of the law courts.

The Symons family went about the daily round, working their ground, tending their livestock and labouring for others. They were probably hardly aware of the dissatisfaction felt by some. On their visits to town they would hear news from other places, brought in by carriers and drovers who passed through when transporting goods and animals to the markets.

Visits into Dorking would have been the highlights of their lives. Only the bed-ridden and the sick failed to go to the annual Ascension Day fair, while for the rest of the year the country folk went to town on Thursdays for the market and on Sundays to attend church.

After the church service they lingered to talk to friends, to join in some festivity appropriate to the church calendar, or to watch sport. Sometimes there might be dancing, or young men practicing leaping and vaulting. There might be a jingling match where blindfold players tried to catch the one who wore jingling bells; occasionally a little pig with a greased tail was produced for people to try to catch, with a prize for the one who could hang onto the pig's tail for the longest time.

Much time is wasted
     now away
At pigeon-holes and
     nine-pin play.
Whilst hob-nail Dick and
     simp'ring Frances
Trip it away in country
     dances:
At stool-ball and at barley
     brake,
Wherewith they harmless
     pastime make.

    Anon.

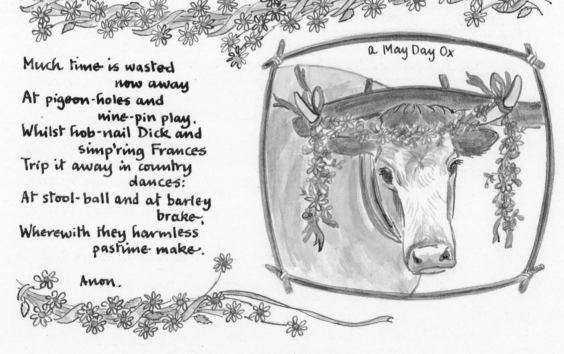

a May Day Ox

Since 1627 there was a law forbidding all waggoners, carters, drovers and other such people from travelling on Sundays on pain of a 20 shillings fine if they were caught, so that the Lord's Day should be properly observed.

A Game-cock with feathers trimmed for fighting.

A Pair of Cock-fighting Spurs. The leather band was bound round the cock's leg with twine. The natural spur passed through the hole.

At this time there were about a hundred dwellings in Dorking, and it had a busy market with a handsome market hall in the main street as well as a corn market.

People came from long distances for Dorking's specialty, which was poultry. The market was gaining a reputation for fine capons, and it was to become one of the most famous in England for table birds.

Many yoemen's and husbandmen's wives round Dorking, and particularly to the south of the town across the Holmwood, through Capel, Ockley, Newdigate, and way on to Horsham over the Sussex border, reared the five-toed breed of DORKING FOWL. When cock birds were caponised they grew into enormous and succulent table birds, weighing up to six pounds.

39

The OWL IS ABROAD, The BAT and The TOAD, and so is The NOLE SIT BOTH in A NOLE AND FROG

Hag Stone : a stone with a natural hole through it was hung in byres and stables to deter witches from milking cows at riding cows and horses overnight and returning them exhausted in a "hag-ridden" condition.

Hag Stones were also used by grooms, carters and ostlers as charms to assist mares in foaling and to ward off general misfortune

BEN JOHNSON · THE WITCHES' CHARM

F·R·M

CHARLES 1ST

He dispensed with Parliament for much of the time and ruled the country without it. He levied several unpopular taxes and the ordinary people felt he had little regard for them.

He enclosed Richmond Park for his own use and evicted all the tenants from it, making them homeless and landless.

By the early 1640's there was once more a Parliament. It declared King Charles's taxes were illegal and Acts were passed that prevented his ruling without a Parliament again. Parliament had managed to diminish the King's powers.

Charles I's quarrels and negotiations with Parliament continued until August 1642 when it was clear that peaceful persuasion could not resolve their differences and Charles raised his standard at Nottingham.

The CIVIL WAR had begun.

THE KING
was supported by Royalists or Cavaliers, a name adapted from the Spanish "cavaliero", the Papist horse-soldier of Spain. Generally they were noblemen or country gentlemen.

PARLIAMENT
was supported by the Roundheads, so called because some of them wore their hair cut short. Generally they were from the large towns, London and south-east England.

Most Royalists believed the king to be Head of the Church and as such a sacred personage. Many who sided with Parliament also held this view. There was a section of Parliamentary Protestants who were more zealous and strict in their religion than the rest. For them loyalty to God took precedence over loyalty to the King. These were the Puritans.

Thus religion became a major issue in splitting the country with Protestants, including Puritans, on the side of Parliament, and those who were not as serious in their religion and who enjoyed recreations on Sunday on the side of the King.

JULY 1644

In July 1644 the Battle of Marston Moor took place in Yorkshire. The Puritan officer who was instrumental in winning the battle for Parliament was OLIVER CROMWELL who was shortly to rise to much greater fame.

Meanwhile at the cottage on the edge of Holmwood Comon THOMAS SYMONS was mourning the death of his wife: ANN. She was buried on 15 July 1644 leaving a son THOMAS, age 19 and a daughter JANE, age 16

The county of Surrey was largely on the side of Parliament, but the fighting mostly took place in the north and west of England.

Important gun-powder mills were situated in Surrey, and the three counties of Surrey, Sussex and Kent contained the major works where canon were made, thus the king was deprived of ammunition.

42

The **CIVIL WAR** continued, with battles being fought in various parts of England. Sometimes invading Scots armies were involved.

As the Royalist strongholds surrendered one by one, divisions of religion began to emerge amongst the Parliamentarians. The Presbyterian faction became stronger, while Oliver Cromwell was the leader of the Independents, who followed Puritan ideals.

In 1646 the King's armies in the north were defeated by Scots armies. The Scots tried to convert the King to the Presbyterian religion, but he refused to take the Covenant, believing that the Scots would support him in any case against the Independents. However towards the end of 1646 the Scots handed the King over to Parliament.

The King escaped from his prison in Newmarket, but in November 1647 he went to the Isle of Wight, hoping to obtain a ship. The governor of Carisbrooke Castle was a Parliamentarian, and the King was held in prison there, awaiting Cromwell's instructions.

The Civil War checked progress in **FARMING**.

The value of manuring land had by now become apparent, but no attention was paid to pasture land.

Ploughs were heavy and cumbrous and usually drawn by oxen. An Act was passed preventing ploughing by tying the tail of an animal to the plough.

Seed was broadcast by hand from the hopper: such as wheat, rye, barley, oats and "codware," or bean crops.

Turnips were grown in gardens. Their value as winter feed for sheep and cattle had not been realised.

Potatoes were occasionally grown in gardens but were regarded as luxuries. There was no attempt at this time to improve breeds of cattle and sheep.

Some thought wastes and commons should be enclosed and properly cultivated, but this would have deprived cottagers of space on which to keep a cow. One writer declared: "people are no where more penurious than such as border on commons.

There was resistance by husband-men to trying anything new; "new seeds will not grow here with us, for our forefathers never used them."

43

For forty years our royal throne
Has been his father's and his own
Nor is there any one but he
With right can there a sharer be;
For who better may Our high sceptre sway
Than he whose right it is to reign?
Then look for no peace, For the wars will never cease
Till the king enjoys his own again

February 1648

Two good men of Reigate, 6 miles from Dorking, were murdered by Parliamentary troops that were quartered there. Many people were injured. Local people were obliged to house the troops free of charge.

8 May 1648

Local people, master and servant alike went into Dorking for a meeting. The people could not tolerate the troops any longer, nor the disturbance of ministers in their churches, and they wanted the old laws back again, along with the restoration of King Charles, if he would come to terms with Parliament. They did not want Cromwell and his Puritan ideals, despite the fact that most Surrey people had previously backed Parliament. At the Dorking meeting a petition was drawn up in preparation for carrying to Parliament.

16 May 1648

There was a great gathering from all over Surrey at eight in the morning on Putney Heath, of all those intending to accompany the Petition to London. Each man was given a green and white riband to set upon his hat so that the City Corporation should know which had been given permission to march.
They marched crying: "God and King Charles! Hey for King Charles", first to the House of Lords then to the House of Commons. At the House of Commons the throng were kept waiting for a tediously long time and everyone grew restless and began to shout: "Bring back the old ways, the old laws and the old rights!" The guards set upon them and some Petitioners were wounded and killed, others scattered and escaped.

At this time THOMAS SYMONS JUNIOR was twenty two years old, and it is quite possible that he, and perhaps his father too, went to the meeting in Dorking and accompanied the Petition to Parliament

JANUARY 1649 King Charles I was brought from Carisbrooke Castle, through Farnham in Surrey and from thence to London for trial by a special Court of Justice

THE KING WAS FOUND GUILTY OF HIGH TREASON AND CONDEMNED TO THE SCAFFOLD.

The king believed that his right to be sovereign was a God-given Trust.

KING CHARLES IST WAS BEHEADED ON TUESDAY 30TH JANUARY 1649.

After the execution England became a COMMONWEALTH, ruled by a body of men: the Council of State, with Oliver Cromwell as its Chairman.

For the following eleven years life in England was changed. The days were taken up with work and prayer and most of the old entertainments and pastimes were unlawful. On the sabbath a gloom descended over the entire population that had, in former years, been capering in fun and sport upon village greens all over the country.

In 1649 a SURVEY of the MANOR was carried out for the lords of the Manor: the Right Honourable Henry Howard, Earl of Arundel, who owned three quarters of it, and the Right Worshipful Sir Ambrose Brown, who owned one quarter.

At this time the HOLMWOOD COMMON extended to 796 acres. To the east, beyond Anstiebury Camp up in the hills, MOUNTHEATH COMMON, was 113 acres, and to the north of Dorking, ASHCOMBE HEATH was 219 acres.

The land that the yeomen held, either copyhold or freehold, was usually scattered across the manor and was not all in one compact block. Some of the neighbouring properties to Betchett Green were held by:
William Palmer - NYES and WIGGONS   Sir George Sondes - REDLANDS
John Heather - MARYFIELDS   Thomas Young - BREAKSPEARS, TURNERS
Edward Nettlefold - LIME PITS   Mary Swan - BREGSELLS   Thomas Wright - HYLD
Richard Constable - SPROTS   Richard Box - KITLANDS   Will. Pilfold - MYNOCK WOOD

Here at the fountain's sliding foot,
Or at some fruit-tree's mossy root,
Casting the body's vest aside—,
My soul into the boughs does glide;
There, like a bird, it sits and sings
Then whets and combs its silver wings,
And, till prepared for longer flight,
Waves in its plumes the various light.

Andrew Marvell 1621-1678

Come and trip it, as you go,
On the light fantastic toe—;
And in thy right hand lead with thee
The mountain-nymph sweet Liberty;
And if I give thee honour due,
Mirth admit me of thy crew,
To live with her and live with thee
In unreproved pleasures free;

John Milton 1608~1674

Leith Hill   Camp   Anslie   Redlands
Wynickwood
Swyres
Stoney Street   Skempe
Moorhurst   Shute
Maryfield
Nyes   Belchett
Green
Wiggons

Holmwood Common

WEST FROM THE COMMON

A Diagrammatic
Representation

FR–PA

Reference:
Survey Map. 1649

During the Commonwealth the people were allowed to travel only to church on Sunday and were not permitted to make a journey anywhere else. No one could enter an inn, take lodging, or drink or smoke in a tavern, sell anything, dance, sing or play an instrument. A woman was not supposed to sew, spin, launder, or even to dry clothes on a Sunday.

During the Commonwealth weddings were strictly civil ceremonies performed by a Justice of the Peace.

Jane and Edward's wedding was conducted by Samuel Rowse of Great Bookham, but where-abouts it took place is not known. Afterwards a Registrar appointed by the Government recorded the marriage in St. Martin's, Dorking, parish registers.   It would have been a simple wedding compared with that of Jane's parents before the Civil War for the Puritan regime did not approve of celebrations. Probably Jane had a small party.

In 1656 a son, Edward, was born to Edward and Jane Piper.

The baby grew to manhood and marriage.

ON 15ᵀᴴ NOVEMBER 1657 JANE PIPER WAS BURIED.

The register does not record if she died in childbirth. In 1661 her husband married the widow of a gentleman. In 1662 Edward Piper himself died.

1655 Jane Symons

was 27 years old, and for a husbandman's daughter, she made a good marriage —

9ᵗʰ October 1655 JANE married EDWARD PIPER Barber-chirurgeon of Dorking.

Barber-Surgeons were licenced by the Barber Surgeons Company. They were inferior in status to physicians.

Besides hairdressing and shaving they drew teeth and attended to wounds and broken bones.

Letting blood was the great cure-all for many indispositions, and leeches were much used for blood-sucking. To relieve them of the blood so that they could be used again they were put in salt.

Hirudo medicinalis.

For Good Health: a perfect balance of the four humours of the body ~ blood, phlegm, choler and melancholy

The day that OLIVER CROMWELL died : 3rd September 1658 was marked by severe gales which swept across the country.

The weather on the day of the Lord Protector's going from this world matched the effect the man himself had had upon the country. People believed that God had willed the weather to match the man on that day.

MAY DAY 1660 was a merry day for England for soon the country would have a

King again. Church bells rang, bonfires were lit, old country dances revived, and healths were drunk and drunk again. Later that month, Charles, age 30, son of Charles I, arrived in England from exile

CHARLES II was crowned on 23rd APRIL 1661

On this day there was a severe thunderstorm in the Dorking area, which all but demolished the farm of William Weller of Capel.

In that same year, on 15 October 1661, THOMAS SYMONS, the elder, a widower for 17 years since Ann died, and now aged 71, married again. His new wife was MARY ARNOLD. Mary was probably aged 49, a spinster who had been born in Mickleham, a village about two miles north of Dorking where there were several Arnold families: Arnolds of the Pound, of Westhumble, of the Chequer, and of the Green.

THOMAS SYMONS and MARY lived in the house at Betchett Green
with THOMAS SYMONS, junior. They probably hired a servant girl
to help with the poultry, milk, and domestic work.
By now they would sleep on feather or flock beds with feather
pillows. The old horn beakers were set aside for use in the
buttery, and they drank from pewter mugs instead, but it is
not likely that they were wealthy enough to own a set of
pewter plates, and they still ate off wooden trenchers.

THOMAS SYMONS, junior, now termed himself a "Yeoman".
He was aged 35
With his old father now well cared for by Mary he, himself,
took a bride. Her name was SARAH, but it is not known
when or where the couple were married. It is likely that
both the old and the young couple lived together in the house.

THOMAS
SYMONS
=
SARAH

WATER SOUCHY
a local recipe

Take 2 or 3 flounders and stew with parsley roots
and leaves and 30 peppercorns in 1 quart of water.
Stew until the fish falls to pieces.
Pulp through a sieve.
Set the fish and the liquor it was stewed in over a fire, and
add some perch, tench or flounder and some fresh roots and leaves
of parsley.
Simmer until done well enough and serve in a deep dish with some
bread and butter.

SURREY COURT SESSIONS

The SESSIONS were held every quarter. Sometimes they were in Croydon, sometimes in Reigate, Guildford, Kingston-upon-Thames, or Dorking.

A GRAND JURY of 24 men was drawn from within the county. In Surrey no particular qualifications were required for jurymen, but they usually held lands which were worth at least 20 shillings per annum

THOMAS SYMONS was issued with a writ of Venire Capias to attend the Court Sessions in Croydon in JANUARY 1662.

At that time of the year the journey of about 20 miles, and staying away from home would have been an arduous excursion for a man of his age. Thomas Symons, the elder, was the copyholder; it is likely he was the one that was bidden to be a juryman.

No doubt he would have travelled with other local men: Thomas Hill, Robert Peter, John Lovedale, John Bradbelt, William Warner and William Edwards.

The Court assessed servants' and labourers' wages, assessed the Parishes for charitable purposes and recorded the current prices for ale and soap.

There were not many serious crimes in Surrey. Those prosecuted were ale-house keepers operating without licences, persons playing unlawful games, swearers, scolding women, those selling bread under the Assise, etc. Punishment for such cases constituted of the cocking stool for scolds, the pillory for bakers, or being whipped until the body bled once, twice, or three times, according to the judge's discretion — this for larceny.

When Thomas Symons was a juryman Dorking people had been quite law-abiding over the previous three months. Only Thomas Bothill, brewer of Dorking appeared. He had sold 3 barrels of strong beer for other than domestic use to William Wonham, a victualler, also of Dorking. Wonham had sold the beer, as an ale-house keeper, although he had no licence.

At every Sessions in these times the recusants were summoned to appear. They were mostly Quakers who held their own meetings and did not attend the parish churches. They were summoned for not being in church "in an orderly and sober manner during the time of common prayer for twenty Sundays" prior to the date of the Court.

The Surrey Court was not hard on these men, and fined them 3s 4d each when it could have requested up to 20 shillings.

Thomas Symons would have been acquainted with several of the recusants who lived in his area: Richard, Thomas and Henry Bax, all yeomen, John Stedman and Richard Bourne of Ockley, and John Palmer, carpenter of Capel.

Sessions concluded with the granting of licences— only to married men, house-holders over 30 years old, for being badgers, kidders, carriers, buyers or corn or grain transporters.

18 DECEMBER 1663 THOMAS and SARAH SYMONS' first child, a girl called SARA was christened at St. Martin's Church, Dorking.

It is possible that the local mid-wife, ELIZABETH HOOKER, attended at the birth.

Elizabeth Hooker was occasionally summoned to the County Court Sessions to give evidence in cases where women had borne bastard children.

For instance, in 1661 she had given evidence for MARY BROWN who had given birth to a bastard maiden child. The mother had called out in her labour pains that EDWARD SANFORD, a tallow chandler of Dorking was the father. Elizabeth Hooker also attested that Edward Sanford had begotten another maiden child on the body of widow ELEANOR PRIOR, "having carnal knowledge of her seven nights before Christmas."

In the first case the Court ordered Edward Sanford to pay 18 pence of lawful money of England monthly to the Overseers of the Poor towards relief for Mary Brown's child until it "cometh of age of eight years, then £5 to putting out of child to be an apprentice."

6 NOVEMBER 1665 THOMAS and SARAH SYMONS' second child, a boy called THOMAS was christened at St. Martin's Church, Dorking.

Thus this baby was the third to be called Thomas Symons to live at the house at Betchett Green, and he was the fourth generation of the family there.

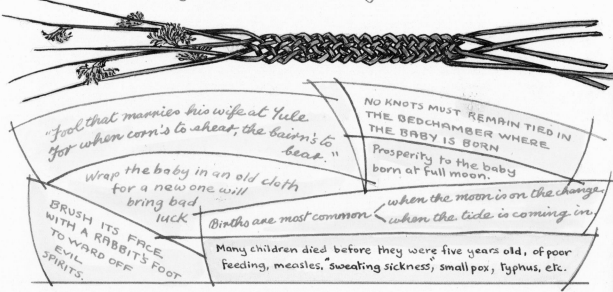

"Fool that marries his wife at Yule For when corn's to shear, the bairn's to bear."

NO KNOTS MUST REMAIN TIED IN THE BEDCHAMBER WHERE THE BABY IS BORN

Prosperity to the baby born at full moon.

Wrap the baby in an old cloth for a new one will bring bad luck

Births are most common ⟨ when the moon is on the change, when the tide is coming in.

BRUSH ITS FACE WITH A RABBIT'S FOOT TO WARD OFF EVIL SPIRITS.

Many children died before they were five years old, of poor feeding, measles, "sweating sickness," small pox, typhus, etc.

1665 PLAGUE IN LONDON

The year that Sarah Symons was carrying her baby Thomas there occurred what came to be known as the Great Plague of London.

From August to September people in London died in great numbers. One seventh of the population died.

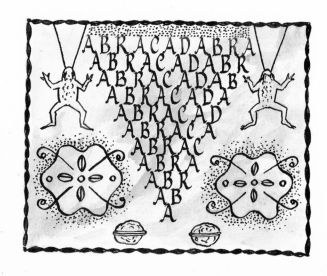

No one knew how they caught the plague and there were many superstitions and amulets that were supposed to prevent it, such as carrying a walnut filled with mercury, or wearing a dried toad's head or a hare's foot on a string round the neck, or taking a pill of turpentine every morning.

The Plague was actually transmitted by infected fleas that were carried by rats. The mortality rate was 90% for those that caught it, with death, or recovery, within a few days of the onset of fever and sickness. This was followed by swellings in the groin, armpits and neck, then delirium and coma.

1666 FIRE OF LONDON

After a bitterly cold winter when the Thames froze over there was a terrible gale on February 3rd, when houses in London blew down.

June saw the start of a very hot and dry summer, with drought beginning on June 27th. Although, through the summer there had been a few thunderstorms here and there, by September all was dry, crisp and dusty.

On September 3rd fire broke out in London city, and fanned by strong east winds, rapidly spread. The City was almost all destroyed, including old St. Paul's Cathedral, medieval churches, and thousands of timber and plaster dwellings.

The drought broke on September 19th

The fire raged for four days.

THOMAS SYMONS, the elder, must have begun to feel his age at last, for in 1668, when he was aged 78, he decided to pass the Copyhold of the house on to his son Thomas.

Thus, on 24 January 1668 THOMAS SYMONS, junior, was admitted to the copyhold at the meeting of the Court Baron.

from the Court Rolls.

THOMAS SYMONS, the elder, had another year and a half to live. He died at the age of 80 and was buried at St. Martin's Church on 2nd August 1670

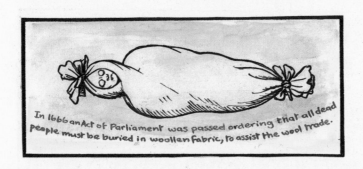

In 1666 an Act of Parliament was passed ordering that all dead people must be buried in woollen fabric, to assist the wool trade.

By this time there was another young Symons at Betchett Green: John, christened May 1668. He was followed by Richard, 1671. The last one seems to have been William, christened 27 December 1674 followed by another famine year in 1674, with wheat at 68s 8d per quarter.

1673 ~ A famine year, with a poor harvest and large numbers of cattle and sheep dying due to continual wet weather

THE COMMON

Without the facilities of the Common many people would not have been able to manage. The men cut turves and bracken in season. While they watched their sheep, cattle and geese, the women collected firewood or spun wool on the distaffs they always carried with them. The animals grazed, fought, mated, were born, caught diseases and died.

The Common was a place of rivalries, fights, friendship, for people and animals alike. Some gentlemen believed it would have been better if all commons were enclosed and cultivated, saying that they were "nurseries of idleness and breeding grounds for thieves and horse stealers".

From the Holmwood Common's highest places there could be seen a ridge which filled almost all the northern horizon. Quarries had been cut in parts of it, and the white chalk gleamed in the sun. The ridge ran from Reigate at its eastern end to the high reaches of Ranmore Common on the west. A deep cleft in the ridge, at Box Hill, was where the River Mole ran through on its way to the Thames, but this was hidden from the Common by an intermediate hill, which also hid Dorking town from view.

In July 1662 the Court Session Rolls recorded: "The highway at the south end of Homewood leading from Dorking to Capell has been so out of repair.....that the king's liege people.....cannot pass without great danger to their common nuisance. The inhabitants of Dorking ought to make repair the same whenever necessary".

OCTOBER 1672 • COURT LEET: Thomas Symons, along with Henry Swan from Bregsells, John Dibble, Edwin Hooker, John Seaman and Henry Gosden, were all brought before the Court for keeping **GOATS** on the Holmwood. Goats were not commonable animals. All the men were ordered to remove the goats from the Common before the next Feast of St. Andrew the Apostle, or else a fine of 20 shillings would be imposed on each of them.

1678

A VERY HOT DRY SUMMER & AUTUMN

Three generations of the SYMONS family: JOHN, THOMAS senior and THOMAS junior, had held the copyhold and occupied the house at Betchett Green.

In 1678 Thomas appeared at the Court Baron and he was granted a

LICENCE TO DEMISE
(demise = convey, grant by will or lease)

> To this court came Thomas Symonds, customary tenant of this manor and sought a licence to demise all and singular his customary lands and tenements within the aforesaid manor for whatever or to whomsoever he pleases. To hold from the Feast of St. Michael last past for 21 years. And it is granted to him alone by the court, upon paying to the Lords a fine for his licence 7 shillings according to the custom of the manor as aforesaid.

It must have been at this time that Thomas and his family moved, but where they went to is not known, only that they stayed in the area, for further entries appeared in the Dorking Parish Registers.

85 years had passed since the house had been built.

Tom Symons, Sarah, William, Richard, John, Thomas, Sara.

Dorking Market sold good earthenware pottery, corn, and fat poultry.

The area was famous for its strawberry fields.

THE NEW OCCUPIERS

Minnickwood was about a half hour walk away from the Green. It lay on the southern slopes of the hills, with ancient Anstiebury Camp above and Ockley and Capel villages down to the south.

At a cottage at Minnickwood lived "John Pilfold on the Hill", (there was a man of the same name in Capel, too,) with his wife Dorothy and children John and Joane. It seems that "John-on-the-Hill" had a sister Mary, now married, and a brother, WILLIAM, aged about 36. Their father, also William, had died 10 years earlier.

Where WILLIAM PILFOLD lived, or whether he was already married when Thomas Symons agreed to let the house to him is not known. His wife was called SYBILLA, a distinctive name for the time.

Not long after they came to the house William bought the freehold of about 24 acres of mixed arable and woodland called SKEMPE from Edward Nettlefold. It was rated at 3s 1d per annum. Skempe lay beyond the Shute fields that adjoined the house and which were owned by Joseph Young, but it was connected to the Green by a long strip of land down which ran the stream which provided the house with water.

It is likely Skempe was heavy wet ground, for in the hills above were bottomless bogs that drained into it. William probably grew corn, peas and beans, and a patch of flax and hemp, rotating his crops so that part was fallow on the third year.

58

QUAKERS

WILLIAM PILFOLD very likely spent the first part of his life at Minnick-wood, and although it was on a wild hillside where few people passed by, he would have been aware of the Quaker faith since childhood.

A quarter of a mile from Minnickwood lay Kitlands, an old farm house which had been occupied by the Bax family since 1622. The Bax family were amongst the earliest adherents to the Quaker faith. George Fox, who founded the Society of Friends, 1650, had visited Kitlands in 1668. Thomas Bax, who lived there, had, with his brother Richard, been imprisoned for refusing to pay obligatory tithes on their land, payment which they regarded as a relic of the Old Testament Jewish concept, and which was not a command of the Gospel.

BE RICH IN CHARITY   GIVE NO BAD WORDS TO ANYONE   GOD IS IN EVERY MAN

1681 ~ Summer hot and dry, a severe drought in England.

1682 · October ~ Thomas Symons sold the copyhold of Betchett Green to Dorking wheelwright William Hooker.

1683 · March ~ James Wood, yeoman of Dorking was admitted to the copyhold of the property, obtaining it from William Hooker. James Wood was to retain it for nearly 30 years, with the Pilfolds in occupation.

About this time William and Sybilla Pilfold had a daughter, Mary, who became a Quaker. She seems to have been their only child.

1685~1688 THE REIGN OF JAMES II

James was not a popular king. He dismissed Parliament because it would not listen to his schemes for religious toleration, and many people were afraid that he intended to impose the Roman Catholic religion on the country.

In consequence a small group of noble-men invited Prince William of Orange, (son of the eldest daughter of Charles II), and Princess Mary, (who was the Protestant daughter of King James), to come from Holland to England with an army.

THE "GLORIOUS" REVOLUTION

Prince William and Princess Mary met with no resistance. James II fled from London to France. It was a bloodless revolution.

The pair were invited to be king and queen on the presentation of the DECLARATION OF RIGHTS, on 13 February 1689. They accepted. The Declaration was given statuatary right in the BILL OF RIGHTS, which laid down the rule that the king could not cancel or suspend any laws, that he could not keep a standing army in time of peace, nor levy taxes without consent of Parliament, which had to be summoned frequently. There could be no more Catholic monarchs.

The BILL OF RIGHTS transformed the relationship between Parliament and the Crown, and the following ten years saw a further shrinkage of royal authority.

The reign of William and Mary marked the beginning of a new era of religious tolerance with the Act of Toleration, 1689.

AT THIS TIME EACH VILLAGE WAS ISOLATED AND LARGELY SELF SUFFICIENT. COMMUNICATION WAS DIFFICULT, ROADS WERE OFTEN IMPASSABLE EXCEPT FOR A HORSEMAN ON A STRONG HORSE OR A COACH DRAWN BY EIGHT HORSES. EDUCATION DID NOT NORMALLY EXTEND TO THE FARMING CLASSES. THUS IMPROVEMENTS IN AGRICULTURE WERE NEITHER LOOKED FOR NOR EASILY COMMUNICATED.

The people of England, of whom there were about five and a half million, prospered. There were four and a half times as many country-dwellers as there were people who lived in towns, and every country-man had his patch of land on which he could grow a certain amount of his food, if not all of it.

The Pilfolds are not likely to have ranked amongst the better-off farmers. The income William obtained for produce he sold, and for working periodically for other people, probably amounted to about £20 a year. The family would have eaten well, worked hard, suffered no repressions and were fortunate to live at a time when life was kind to country people.

The entire county of Surrey had, over the preceeding 60 years, become rich.

In 1636 Surrey had ranked in eighteenth place in wealth amongst the counties of England. By 1693 it had risen to second place, with Middlesex in first position.

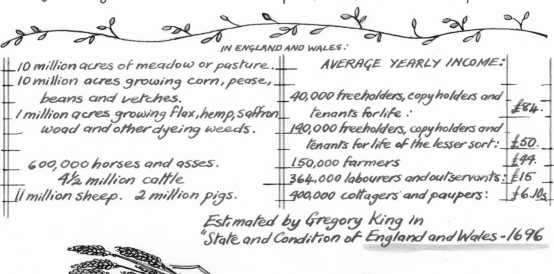

IN ENGLAND AND WALES:

	AVERAGE YEARLY INCOME:	
10 million acres of meadow or pasture.		
10 million acres growing corn, pease, beans and vetches.		
1 million acres growing flax, hemp, saffron, woad and other dyeing weeds.	40,000 freeholders, copyholders and tenants for life:	£84.
	190,000 freeholders, copyholders and tenants for life of the lesser sort:	£50.
600,000 horses and asses.	150,000 farmers	£44.
4½ million cattle	364,000 labourers and outservants:	£15
11 million sheep. 2 million pigs.	400,000 cottagers and paupers:	£6.10s

Estimated by Gregory King in
"State and Condition of England and Wales - 1696

1702 KING WILLIAM died,
(his wife Mary had died earlier.)
QUEEN ANNE, sister of
Mary, was crowned.

War of Spanish Succession began,
to prevent the King of France
from eventually ruling all Europe.

1703 An exceptionally wet
summer. In the autumn there
were fierce storms culminating
in a hurricane on November 26th and 27th. Houses, barns and trees were blown
down. 8000 people lost their lives in floods of the Severn and Thames. Eddystone
lighthouse blew away and twelve warships were sunk off the coast. In
southern England there were more violent gales on December 7th, 8th, 27th, 28th.

1704
The Battle of Blenheim,
in the Danube valley. The Duke of Marlborough led the scarlet clad English
infantrymen and the cavalry against French troops to win the battle which did
much to destroy the confidence of King Louis and his army.

1705, 1706 Dry summers with good harvests and wheat low in price.

> Happy the man whose wish and care
> A few paternal acres bound,
> Content to breathe his native air,
> In his own ground.
>
> Whose herds with milk, whose fields with bread,
> Whose flocks supply him with attire,
> Whose trees in summer yield him shade,
> In winter fire—.
>
> Alexander Pope 1688-1744

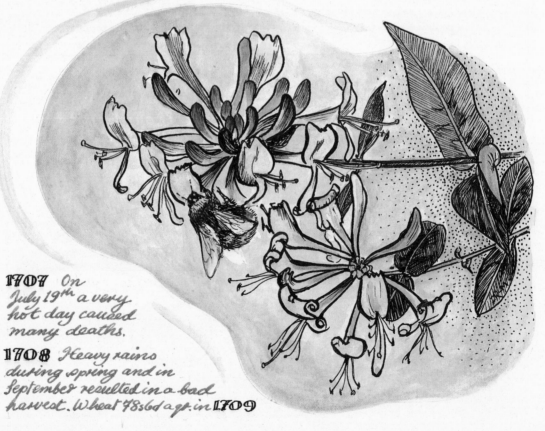

1707 On
July 19th a very
hot day caused
many deaths.

1708 Heavy rains
during spring and in
September resulted in a bad
harvest. Wheat 78s 6d a qr. in **1709**

In the early 1700's there were several young people attending the Friends' meetings, which were held at Kitlands, Pleyestowe farmhouse south of Capel, or in Dorking. At Pleyestowe a piece of ground just inside the gate had been given by a former Richard Bax as a burial place for the Friends.

MARY PILFOLD was one of those walking to the meetings. The Swan family, who had occupied Bregsells farm on the eastern edge of Holmwood Common for more than eighty years, were regular attenders, including Robert Swan and his sister Elizabeth. There was the Peters family too, with Richard Peters and his young brother James. Their father was a hoopshaver.

At the meeting house they would encounter other young people from the district: Richard Bax, who was in his early twenties, and his cousin Nicholas, and Sarah Bax of Ockley Court, who was later to marry Robert Swan.

Mary Pilfold did not find a husband amongst her near neighbours. In 1709 on the 8th of June, and on the 13th July, she and Abraham Tugwell of Ifield, near Crawley, in Sussex, declared their intention to marry (at the Women's Monthly Meeting at Horsham in Sussex, which was about 9 miles from Holmwood).

Abraham Tugwell was forty-three years old, the youngest son of John and Elener Tugwell of Ifield.

> This Day Abraham Tugwell of Ifield and Mary Pilfold did the first time declare their Intentions of takeing each other in Marriage whereupon this Meeting Doth Appoint Jane Garton and Jane Humphry to Enquire of their Clearnes from all others on that Account and bring their Answer to the next Meeting

from the Minutes of the Horsham Meeting.

MARY PILFOLD of Dorking and ABRAHAM TUGWELL made their solemn declaration of marriage at Ifield on 26th July 1709 before the other Friends who were assembled at the meeting.

Back at Betchett Green WILLIAM PILFOLD did not long survive his daughter's departure. Sometime between July 1709 and December 1710 he died. Where he was buried is not known.

His widow SYBILLA remained living in the house.

1710 Shortly after William Pilfold died the owner of the property: JAMES WOOD, decided to sell it.

On 6th December 1710 RICHARD PETERS, hoopshaver, of Dorking, became the copyholder of:

"ALL THAT CUSTOMARY MESSUAGE OR TENEMENT, BARN, STABLE, BUILDINGS, GARDEN, ORCHARD, YARD AND LANDS WITH THE APPURTENANCES THERE—UNTO ······ FORMERLY IN THE OCCUPATION OF WILLIAM PILFOLD (DECEASED) AND NOW IN THE OCCUPATION OF SYBILLA PILFOLD (WIDOW)······"

SIGNATURE of JAMES WOOD COPIED FROM A MEMORANDUM of 1710 RELATING TO THE HOUSE.

It would appear that Sybilla stayed for at least another nine years.

RICHARD PETERS · HOOPSHAVER

Richard Peters had two sons: RICHARD, jnr. and JAMES.

RICHARD, junior was twenty-two years old. The Quakers taught their children to read and write, and, judging by the records, Richard appears to have been an able young man and an ardent Friend. He was, perhaps, his father's favourite of the brothers.

On 27th April 1711 Richard Peters, junior, married Elizabeth Swan of Bregsells at Pleyestowe, and the following month the newly married couple were witnesses to the marriage at Pleyestowe of Elizabeth's brother Robert Swan to Sarah Bax.
Also a witness at this wedding was a twenty-four year old woman who had been born in Charlwood, and who was eventually to join the Peters family. Her name was SARAH ELISS.

JAMES was fourteen years old. He seems to have been a poor scholar who was not very active for the Friends, and was overshadowed by his older brother.

Richard Bourne   Edward Bax
Richard Bax   Rich. Peters sen. Tho. Bax
Edward Bax   Nathaniel Bax John Wall
gun.   ES
Resta Patching   Thomas Bax

COPY OF SIGNATURES FROM MEETING BOOK 1719

HOOPMAKING

Richard Peters, senior, had followed his father into the hoopshaving business, and it was a business which was growing. With an expanding population in England, more and more goods were needed and these were despatched all over the country by pack horses and waggons. Many of these commodities were packed into barrels that were hooped by withies that had been cleaved and shaven by men such as Richard Peters working in the copses of south-eastern England.

Hoopshaving was a winter occupation, with the men working in the woods only from Michaelmas until Lady Day. In summer time they worked their own land, or laboured for others.

Once the techniques of hoopmaking had been mastered and the chest muscles had become accustomed to the tension that continually drawing the shave down the rods generated, there was plenty of time for a man to think. Richard Peters would probably have thought mostly of his business, his neighbours, his religion and his children. He made money not only from the hoops themselves, but from the by-products, such as shavings for thatching, while chips and small shavings were dried to make firelighters for selling in towns.

1719

A COPY OF HER SIGNATURE.

Sarah Elis

Young JAMES PETERS followed his father in the hoopshaving business and in 1719, when he was twenty-three years old, he and SARAH ELISS, who had originally come from Charlwood and who was almost ten years older than he was, decided to marry.

On 4th May a small party of people walked across the Holmwood Common towards Dorking, where a Friend's Meeting House had been built ten years before, utilising the timbers from the frame of an old demolished house.

James and Sarah were going to the meeting to declare their intention to marry, their parents having given their consent. Sarah's father was dead, but according to the report of the meeting, her mother was present.

Copy of report of monthly meeting 4 May 1719

James Peter of Dorking hoop maker (Sone of Richd Peter Senr of ye Do Parish Hoop maker) & Sara Elis Spinster of ye Same Pish Daughter of Tho, Elis of late of Charlewood husbondman Deceased did this day declare there intentions of taking each other in Marridge, there parence (Living) being present did give there consent thy meeting doth apoint Rich: Bowne & Robt Swan to inquire into there Cleernes and make report to the next monthly meeting

The following month, on 3rd June, the couple attended a meeting at Kitlands where they declared their continued intentions, and neither Richard Bourne nor Robert Swan had been able to discover a reason why they should not marry.

The WEDDING itself took place on 15th June 1719 at Pleyestowe. That year the summer was hot and dry.

Sarah Eliss would have worn a freshly laundered dress, which, like her bonnet, was old and outmoded. The Quakers did not change their clothes according to the fashions of the time; fashions which they considered to be but vanities. They were taught that their attire should reflect a quiet and meek spirit.

The meeting began with a period of silence and then one of the Friends rose to explain the wedding procedure.

James and Sarah stood before the assembly and James made his declaration: "I, James Peters, take this my friend Sarah Eliss to be my wife, promising to be unto her a faithful and loving husband with the Lord's assistance, until it shall please the Lord to separate us by death."

Then Sarah declared: "I, Sarah Eliss, take this my friend James Peters to be my husband, promising to be unto him a faithful wife with the Lord's assistance until it shall please the Lord to separate us by death."

Sarah did not receive a wedding ring, for the Quakers regarded the giving of rings as a form of outward show that signified nothing.

Over thirty people were at the meeting to sign James and Sarah's wedding certificate, several of them having made the journey over from Charlwood.

After a period of silence and prayers the elders shook hands and the meeting closed.

IT SEEMS VERY LIKELY THAT JAMES AND SARAH PETERS BEGAN THEIR MARRIED LIFE AT BETCHETT GREEN ALTHOUGH OLD SYBILLA PILFOLD WAS STILL ALIVE. SHE HAD PROBABLY VACATED IT AND WAS CARED FOR BY RELATIONS

HOME IMPROVEMENTS

Once JAMES and SARAH PETERS were installed in the house at Betchett Green it seems likely that at this time improvements were made to it.

Crumbling damp plaster would have been removed from the walls and brick infilling put in its place between the sound timbers.

It was becoming the custom in south-eastern England to hang tiles against the outer walls especially against the upper-storeys, to protect them from the weather. At about this time the southern and western sides of the house were tile-hung on the upper storey.

The ground floor was, literally, the ground. The bare earth would have been strewn with rushes by old Sybilla Pilfold, who renewed them every year, or, as she grew old, probably laid a few fresh ones on top of the old. It was very likely the Peters family who had stone slabs laid in the buttery and hearth room.

The stone slabs came from Horsham, in Sussex, where it was dug from quarries there. Many houses in the Horsham area were roofed with this stone, having small slabs at the ridge and grading to large ones at the eaves. The stone was very hard wearing. Often slabs of it were marked with fossil shapes, or they might be rippled like sand on a river bed.

Riddle:—
Black within and red without;
Four corners round about?
(A chimney).

1727

(In 1714 Queen Anne died and George, Elector of Hanover, who was a descendant of James I was proclaimed King. He understood very little English.

Robert Walpole became the head of government and the King's Prime Minister, and this position has continued to the present day.)

In 1727 King George I died and was succeeded by George II

At this time malt for beer had become very expensive and many people could not afford to drink beer any more.

Gin, nicknamed "Madame Geneva", was cheap and was drunk by many. It soon caused drunkenness.

Tea was increasingly being imported and drunk by a large section of the population.

A good rush would burn for nearly 1 hour.

RUSH LIGHTS, made by dipping peeled rushes in hot fat — perhaps the scummings of the bacon pot.

A family might use 2,400 lights in the year.

The rush was peeled so as to leave a strip to support the pith.

Siboll Pilfold widdow was Buried the 9th day of June 1727

Old Sybilla Pilfold was buried at Capel Church on 6th June 1727

1729

The weather was notable for thunderstorms and high winds.

JAMES and SARAH PETERS had no children, but they had two nieces: the children of James' brother Richard, junior, and his wife Elizabeth.

In 1725 the property "Palmersland" had been passed to Richard, junior, by his father Richard Peters, but Betchett Green, where James and Sarah lived was still held by Richard, senior.

On 26th August 1729 Richard, junior, was buried at Pleyestowe. It would appear that he had died suddenly, probably from an accident. In the previous month he had signed the Friend's Meeting Book as usual and there was no further reference to him afterwards except to record his burial.

After his death his widow Elizabeth was admitted in her own right to "Palmersland."

The month after Richard, junior, died, Richard, senior, made his will. No doubt he was prompted to do so by his son's untimely death, and the realisation that death might come quickly and unexpectedly.

He willed Betchett Green to James and Sarah for the term of their natural lives.

QUAKERS

did not use the word "you" when speaking to one person, but always "thou." They did not regard anyone as being superior or inferior to themselves; they refused to doff their hats to anyone, or bow, or use flattering words in salutation. No titles, such as Mister or Miss were used.

"The world expects more from Friends than from other people; because you profess more. Therefore you should be more just than others in your words and dealings, more righteous, holy and pure in your lives and conversations, so that your lives and conversations may preach."

George Fox.

70

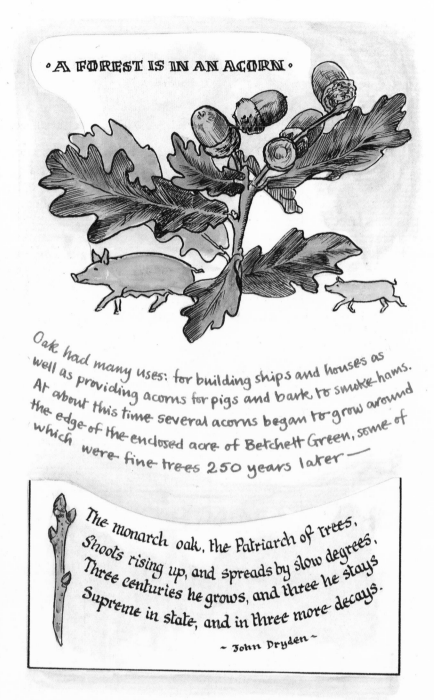

· A FOREST IS IN AN ACORN ·

1730 - There was an excellent harvest.

1733 - The fourth dry year in succession, a very hot summer and a scarcity of winter fodder.

1735 - A severe epidemic of "sheep rot." The sheeps' feet became soft and painful so that they could not stand, they thrived badly and died.

1738 - There was a serious epidemic of influenza in Dorking and a wet May and June helped to increase the cases of "sheep rot".

1739 - War broke out against Spain - a struggle for trade.

1740 - A bitterly cold winter with the cattle dying of cold in stalls. War of Austrian Succession began. Jethro Tull, agricultural innovator & inventor died.

Oak had many uses: for building ships and houses as well as providing acorns for pigs and bark to smoke hams. At about this time several acorns began to grow around the edge of the enclosed acre of Betchett Green, some of which were fine trees 250 years later —

The monarch oak, the Patriarch of trees,
Shoots rising up, and spreads by slow degrees,
Three centuries he grows, and three he stays
Supreme in state, and in three more decays.

~ John Dryden ~

The QUAKERS nowadays lived quiet lives. Most devoted themselves to their businesses, their meetings and their families, which extended to cousins several times removed. They tried to set a good example to others by the way that they lived, but did not try to convert others to their faith. They avoided excess in any form, abided by old habits and customs and were honest in business and prompt in payment of debts.

 **1743** During the drought of JUNE 1743 James Peters' father RICHARD PETERS died.

On Friday, October 20th, James and Sarah went to The Red Lion in Dorking, to attend the Court Baron and it was recorded that:

..."the Court made James Peters of Dorking, aforesaid, yeoman, son of the aforesaid Richard, come, and in his own proper person and produceth and showeth the Steward and Homage aforesaid the last will and testament of the said Richard."....

Part of the will was copied by the Clerk:

"I do by this my last Will and Testament Give and Devise all and singular the said Customary Messuage & Tenement, Barn, Stable, Buildings, Garden, Orchard, Yard and Lands with the appurtenances unto my said son James Peters and Sarah his wife for and during the term of their natural lives and the life of the longer liver of them and from and after the decease of the Survivor of them then I Give and Devise the same unto my deceased's Son Richard Peter's Heirs for ever as in and by the Probate of the said Will it doth appear."

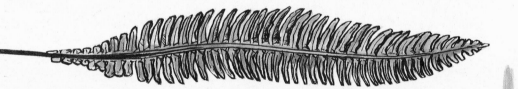

In the 1740's a farm labourer was paid about a shilling a day. There was no work on Sundays. His wife would be paid 10d a day for farm work, and children over the age of seven years could receive 4d a day for farm work.

From 1745 there was a ten year epidemic of rinderpest in cattle.

As the century neared its half-way mark the population of England was increasing everywhere. In Surrey it had grown to 207,000 people: 52,000 more than there had been fifty years before. The country was on the verge of great change, both in the way of life of the people and in the appearance of England itself.

THE NEW 1752 CALENDAR

THE REFORM OF THE CALENDAR CAUSED GREAT CONSTERNATION AMONGST A LARGE SECTION OF THE POPULATION WHO BELIEVED THEY WERE LOSING ELEVEN DAYS OUT OF THEIR LIVES.

The Julian Calendar, invented by Julius Ceasar eighteen centuries before, had been in use, but the year had been too short. The deficit amounted now to eleven days. The Earl of Macclesfield, making a speech in the House of Lords, urged the adoption of the Gregorian Calendar.

THE CHANGE WAS MADE ON SEPTEMBER 2ND. THE FOLLOWING DAY BECAME SEPTEMBER 14TH.

Leaflets had been distributed at Quaker meetings notifying Friends of the change. Everywhere there was much puzzlement. Simple country people thought they were losing eleven days of life and were surprised to find, when they woke up on the morning after September 2nd, that they felt no different in themselves, but still sure that they had somehow been defrauded.
Indeed those lost eleven days did make some differences. For instance the may blossom, which had formerly been in bloom for May Day, did not now appear until the middle of the month.

HORSHAM HANG FAIRS. Sussex criminals were executed at Horsham, which was only 12 miles from Dorking. No doubt many people journeyed to Horsham Common for the entertainment of seeing a hanging. Between 1735 and 1752 forty-three criminals were hanged there: four smugglers, two sheep stealers, six robbers, eight horse-thieves, twelve burglars and eleven murderers.
DORKING had a gallows just outside the town on the lane leading to Coldharbour, but hangings there were rare occasions.

73

YEARS OF CHANGE ～～

In 1755 James and Sarah Peters' sister-in-law Elizabeth Peters died.

In 1756 it was the wettest summer in living memory and this was followed by a famine year, with wheat double the price of two years before.

With bread so expensive the holders of houses and land were obliged to pay more than ever in Poor Rate towards defraying expenses to maintain the poor of the parish.

In 1759 the house & land of James and Sarah Peters   was rated at £3.00   with the rate at 1 shilling · 6 pence in the £ for the half year.

Thus on every Lady Day and Michaelmas Day James paid 4 shillings · 6 pence Poor Rate.

His neighbour, Henry Marsh at Wiggons, was rated at £23.0.0. for his house and land, and paid £1 . 14 shillings . 6 pence Poor Rate every half year.

MEASURES OF CORN

1 peck	≈	2 gallons
8 gallons	≈	1 bushel
2 bushels	≈	1 coomb
2 coombs	≈	1 quarter
5 quarters	≈	1 load or wey
2 loads	≈	1 last

About 2 coombs could be harvested from a quarter of an acre ～

A man could thrash a maximum of 4 bushels of corn in a day ～

A Bushel Measure is 19½ inches diameter and contains 2,218·2 cubic inches ～

1 Bushel of Flour weighs 56 lbs.

The Holmwood people would have been accustomed to churned-up trackways with deep mud in wet weather and hard-baked ruts in dry. The track linking Horsham to Dorking could sometimes be almost impassable for wheeled vehicles.

In 1755 a new turnpike road, a hard road, was begun across Holmwood Common. Eventually it ran from Epsom, southwards through Dorking to Horsham, with a branch to Ockley.

With the new road came many more travellers: on foot, by horseback, in carts, and even in carriages, which had not been able to attempt crossing such rough country before.

Local people were not used to encountering strangers, other than entertainers, gipsies or drovers, and they viewed these new travellers with some suspicion.

Stage Waggons carried both goods and passengers. They travelled about 15 miles a day at 3 miles an hour.

COMMONS all over England were being ENCLOSED, depriving cottagers who had relied on them for their livelihood. After their Common had been fenced off many people were left with nothing but their cottage and a few fowl, and had insufficient land on which to keep animals, and no source for firewood, brushwood, bracken and acorns.

In the SURREY HILLS the land was poor and often too steep to till, thus the hills escaped enclosure, as did the HOLMWOOD COMMON which was boggy and wet, but further out, across the WEALD, commonland was being enclosed.

"From beef without mustard, from a servant who overvalueth herself, from a woman who painteth herself, the Good Lord deliver us." A saying of the time.

DISINTAILMENT • Because James and Sarah Peters had inherited their house by the will of James's father, a special court action had to be brought to enable them to bequeath it or sell it to anyone they wished.

On 26th January 1762, James and Sarah went to the Court Baron at The Red Lion in Dorking with their neighbour Mathew Marsh, a friend called William Biggs, and Thomas Mason, the Headborough of Holmwood.

Very likely the formal court procedure for disintailing the property was inexplicable to all of them. They did and said as instructed. Marsh, Biggs and Mason were all involved, as well as a fictional person called Hugh Hunt.

In the end the property was conveyed to James Peters "in fee simple", (i.e. without limitation to a particular class of heirs), and the court admitted him to the copyhold. James could now do as he liked with the property.

In 1763 James and Sarah borrowed £30 from John Constable, a local yeoman. With the house now disintailed they were able to put it up as security against the loan. The £30, plus interest, was duly paid back at the end of the stipulated six months.

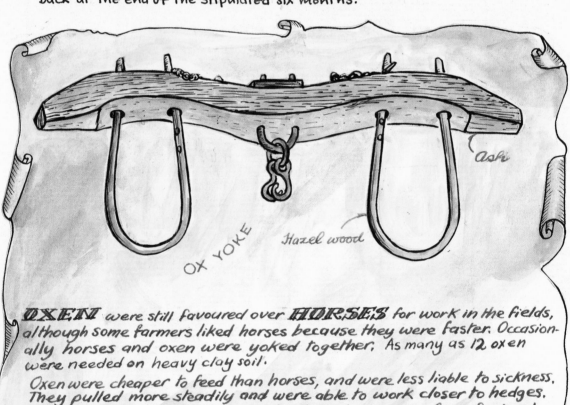

OX YOKE   Hazel wood   ash

OXEN were still favoured over **HORSES** for work in the fields, although some farmers liked horses because they were faster. Occasionally horses and oxen were yoked together. As many as 12 oxen were needed on heavy clay soil.

Oxen were cheaper to feed than horses, and were less liable to sickness. They pulled more steadily and were able to work closer to hedges. Their harness was more simple, their shoeing – on fore-feet only – was cheaper. When past work they were slaughtered for meat.

Nath ʃ. *Wix* — the Contractor for the Poor

A copy of his signature

Workhouses, or Poorhouses became general in the 1730's. The Idea was to set the poor people to work.

Local worthies met periodically at the Parish Church to elect Church Wardens, Surveyors of the Highways, the Constable and the Overseers of the Poor, etc. These were the members of the Parish Vestry.

Before 1765 the Overseers of the Poor for the Dorking Parish Vestry had made contracts with various men over the years to care for the paupers.

In **SPRING 1765** the Overseers engaged a new man called NATHANIEL WIX to look after the paupers in the workhouse. He was paid £420 for the year. The money was to be used at his discretion to pay for the paupers' clothing, food and welfare, while he himself would make his living from the work he set the paupers to do — that is to say: he "farmed the poor."

In **OCTOBER 1765** NATHANIEL WIX bought the copyhold of Betchett Green from JAMES and SARAH PETERS.

Before the property exchanged hands Sarah was "first solely and secretly examined by the said Steward and freely consenting" then Mr. Wix was admitted.

Judging from the Poor Tax books it appears that James and Sarah continued to live in the property; perhaps Mr. Wix had agreed to let them stay there for as long as they lived, while James and Sarah would have enjoyed the money that they received from the sale of the copyhold. They were both old. James was 69 and Sarah was 79. No doubt Mr. Wix felt he would not have long to wait before he could use the property as he wished

There is no failure for the good and wise.
What though thy seed should fall by the wayside,
And the birds snatch it, yet the birds are fed,
Or they may bear it far across the tide
To give rich harvest after thou art dead?

Anon.

In 1766 and 1767 there was an influx of people visiting Dorking to be inoculated against small pox by four surgeons (John Swayne, the elder and the younger, James Swayne and Hugh Kerr), who were operating there. The serum used was of small pox itself, not the cow pox of later times, and as a consequence many people were infected by those that had been inoculated. Nathaniel Wix was granted an extra £1 a head for the inmates of the Poor House who caught the small pox "in the natural way." It was entered in the Vestry minutes that "he has suffered and been at great expense in supporting great numbers of the poor in the parish in the small pox for the last year".

James Peters
yeoman
Born 29. 3rd month (May) 1696
Buried at Pleyestowe
on 31. 5th month (July) 1767
age 71

Sarah Peters
existed for 13 months after James had gone,
and then she closed her last day.
Baptised 23 September 1687 at Charlwood
Buried at Pleyestowe
on 26. 6th month (August) 1768
age 81

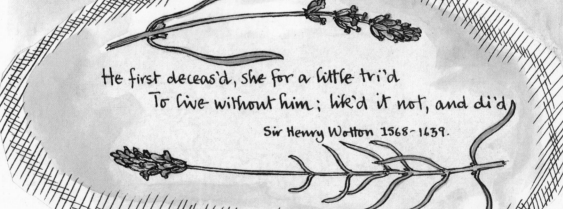

He first deceas'd, she for a little tri'd
To live without him; lik'd it not, and di'd

Sir Henry Wotton 1568-1639.

With James and Sarah Peters dead, Nathaniel Wix looked for a suitable tenant for Betchett Green. He chose **THOMAS ROSE**, an impoverished labourer, age 32 years, with a wife called SARAH and several small children.

At this time in Dorking there was another man, prominent in the town, also with the name Rose. Richard Rose was a wealthy property owner.

It appears that Thomas Rose lived rent free in the house and worked for Nathaniel Wix. Probably he cultivated the ground surrounding the house, growing vegetables and fruit to sell, and for consumption in the Poor House. Nathaniel Wix bought another cottage and pieces of ground, which were, no doubt, cultivated by the paupers.

Down the lane at the farm called "Wiggons" there were changes too. Mathew Marsh's father, Henry, had recently died and Mathew now took the farm on. (The farm was freehold and owned by a William Page, Esq.)
Mathew Marsh was married to Hannah Biggs, and had a little son, Henry, who was sometimes called Biggs, as he had been born before his parents were married.

SMUGGLING

Smuggling was, at this time, common practice.
To avoid the excise goods were landed on the Sussex coast and carried up through Surrey to London.
The smugglers travelled at night by lonely trackways, and the goods were distributed as they went, often to respectable squires and yeomen.

Holmwood people aided and abetted the smugglers. On the highest point of the North Downs, on Leith Hill, a tower folly had been built by a Richard Hill, Esq. in 1766
Smugglers used the tower to signal across the Weald to those with strings of packhorses who were travelling northwards. In Dorking itself there was a warren of caves which may have been used as hiding places for the goods. There were frequent skirmishes between smugglers and Excisemen in the area.

POACHING. In an Act of 1770 anyone convicted of poaching between sunset and sunrise risked 6 month's imprisonment. For a second offence they received one year plus a public whipping.

1770's

In the second half of the century the population of England was increasing and food was expensive.

The Poor became Poorer and the Rich grew Richer.

Cheese, bread and tea was the staple diet of poor people, while dinner in a wealthy house could last for four or five hours with many dishes.

Holmwood Mill was run by Henry Swan.

Many town people now bought ready made bread: either a "wheaten" or a "household" loaf.

In Surrey the average weekly wage was 9 shillings.

TEA leaves were sometimes mixed with blackberry leaves to make them go further. The poor used their tea leaves time and time again and some bought used leaves from wealthy houses. Much tea was brought into the country by smugglers.

Nathaniel Wix continued to renew his contract to farm the the poor and every year the Overseers increased the payment to him for their food and clothing. In June 1774 his allowance was £575 for the following year.

In 1778 there were 48 paupers resident in the Poorhouse and many others were receiving out-relief, including Thomas Rose and his family.

There were many more books being published of the instructional kind, on such subjects as cookery, housekeeping and agriculture.

It may not be amiss to tell the Reader how he may preserve his own Posteriors, as well as the Horse's Back, from galling, fretting or excoriating... ...For when by the Fridging, Etc. in Riding the Serum or watery Part of the Blood is gathered between the two Skins, it is then too late to prevent a sore Backside.

Therefore either apply pretty large Plaisters spread thin upon Leather with *Diachylon* or what is sometimes called *Diapalm* to the Buttocks before you really want them or be content to jog on with a wry Face and a sore Arse.

from The Art of Farriery, Improved

by Henry Bracken, 1773

1780's

1782 ACT OF PARLIAMENT: "Gilbert's Act": Poor people who could not find employment could apply to the Guardians of the Poor, who would be obliged to find work for them to do near their place of abode. The poor people received maintenance and were paid the balance of their wages. As a consequence there was a strain on the parish resources and some poor people did not bother to seek work for themselves.

1783

"The summer of the year 1783 was an amazing and portentous one, and full of horrible phenomena; for besides the alarming meteors and tremendous thunderstorms that affrighted and distressed the different counties of this kingdom, the peculiar haze, or smoky fog, that prevailed for many weeks in this island and in every part of Europe was a most extraordinary appearance, unlike anything known within the memory of man." ----- "All the time the heat was so intense that butcher's meat could hardly be eaten the day after it was killed; and the flies swarmed so in the lanes and hedges that they rendered the horses half frantic and riding irksome."

Gilbert White. The Natural History of Selbourne.

DORKING Town was old and its roads were poorly surfaced. Now that the turnpike road had been constructed Dorking's corn and cattle markets suffered in favour of Horsham.

Lime Kilns by the roadside were a common sight. The lime was carted to acidic fields which had been lying fallow. Furze was cut from nearby common or field to fuel the kilns.

In the late 1700's pheasants, which had been introduced into England from China, began to increase, but they did not become common in the country side until about fifty years later.

1789 Nathaniel Wix received £700 to run the Poor House, £30 of which was for putting poor children to service and clothing them as the Churchwardens and Overseers directed ——

In 1790 MATHEW MARSH, from Wiggons, died, just as the new house he had had built on the Green was finished. Mathew's son, HENRY, who had married MARY RANDALL a few years before, now farmed Wiggons.

In 1792 Britain went to war with France to prevent the coast-line from Calais to the Zuider Zee falling under the control of the French

During the last 30 years there had been a 40% rise in prices. Poor people lived on barley meal, cheese and tea. Those with sufficient land on which to keep a pig were best off, but labourers with large families were usually impoverished.

Land rents were rising rapidly in line with other things. In 1794 wheat stood at 75 shillings 2 pence a quarter.

NATHANIEL WIX decided to give up farming the poor, despite the Overseers begging him to reconsider. He owned a small house on Butterhill in Dorking and probably planned to retire there.

He gave THOMAS ROSE notice to quit from Betchett Green, for he wanted a tenant who would pay him rent until he was able to find a buyer for the copyhold. The ROSE family had been in occupation for about 22 years, so leaving was probably a blow to them. THOMAS was about fifty years old. However he went to work for local landowner JOHN TILT, who also provided him with a cottage on the Holmwood.

NATHANIEL WIX found a tenant for Betchett Green in JAMES EDE, a man of middle years, who had married ALICE IRELAND. It would appear that they had lived in their new abode for only a few days when their baby son, Thomas, died

Time went by and Nathaniel Wix could not find a buyer for the copyhold. Perhaps he was not in the best of health and did not want to go on looking for one himself, because on 17th November 1796 he "did out of Court Surrender into the hands of William James, gentleman, Deputy Steward, and authorised him to take the Surrender."

Nathaniel Wix lived for another year, and died in December 1797, two months after a buyer for the copyhold of Betchett Green had been found by the Duke of Norfolk's Court Steward.

Butterhill.

A cottage lone and still,
  With bowers nigh,
Shadowy, my woes to still
  Until I die—.
Such pearl from Life's fresh crown
Fain would I shake me down.
Were dreams to have at will,
This would best heal my ill,
  This would I buy.

Thomas Lovell Beddoes
1803–1849

Thanksgiving for Plenty. O Most Merciful Father, who of thy gracious goodness hast heard the devout prayers of thy Church and turned our dearth and scarcity into cheapness and plenty; We give thee humble thanks for this thy special bounty; beseeching thee to continue thy loving-kindness unto us, that our land may yield us her fruits of increase, to thy glory and our comfort; through Jesus Christ our Lord
Amen.

Dorking } to wit
of Surrey

The Court Baron of The
Earl of Arundel and Surrey Herioditore
aforesaid there holden in and for the said
in the thirty Eighth Year of the Reign o
One thousand seven
there.

30th Oct 1797

At th
day of
it fu
same
hard
Colmw
ce of
n hel
Path
ises
the s
s for
A
stead or a
to his Use
ard

and thereupo
six Nath
Gentleman
at Custoina
situat
fore in
mises th
e thousar
Privilege
Claim and
hoof of
de that i
any other pe
same out of

And upon Henry Marsh in his
mitted tenant of the Lord of this Manor to the aforesaid Messuage an
tenances so Surrendered to his use as aforesaid And thereupon the L
doth now at this Court grant the same to the said Henry Marsh So
ad assigns for ever of the Lord of this Manor by the Rod and by Copy of
of this Manor by the Yearly Rent of Eight pence Heriot fealty Suit of Court
Tight accustomed And so the said Henry Marsh is now Admitted Tenan
d doth his ffealty and he giveth and payeth to the Lord in Court fo
ngin.

84

THE NEW OWNER OCCUPIER

Henry Marsh

A COPY OF HIS SIGNATURE.

HENRY MARSH was an only child, who had been taught to read and write; this set him above many of his neighbouring farmers.

At the age of nineteen, in 1786, he had married Mary Randall, who was already with child. The son, Mathew, was born three months after the wedding, but he soon died. Eventually Henry and Mary had other children.

After his father, Mathew Marsh died, Henry ran "Wiggons," but it seemed he did not prosper. He left "Wiggons" and moved to a more modest property. At the end of 1796 the Poor Rate Book indicates that Nathanial Wix's under-tenant James Ede moved out of Betchett Green and Henry Marsh moved in, but it was not until October 1797 that Henry was actually admitted to the copyhold at Court.

Only two years later Henry Marsh was in difficulties again. At the Court Baron held at The Red Lion in Dorking on 10 January 1799, he put up his home as security against a loan of £50 from local yeoman John Stedman

".. this Surrender is upon this Condition nevertheless that, if the said Henry Marsh, his Heirs, Executors, Administrators or Assigns or any of them do and shall well and truly pay or cause to be paid unto the said John Stedman his Executors Administrators or Assigns the full sum of Fifty Pounds of lawful money of Great Britain upon the Tenth Day of July next ensuing the same after the Rate of Five Pounds for One Hundred Pounds for a year without any deduction or abatement whatever then this Surrender to be void or else remain in force....."

1799

turned out to be a miserable year. It was cold and wet from January right through to December. From June 22nd to November 17th there were only eight days without rain. The harvest was a disaster, the fallow fields and turnip fields were seas of mud.

No doubt better men than Henry Marsh despaired. He could not raise the £50 plus the interest when it became due, and his home was forfeit.

The Surrey Union Hunt was formed.

The Nineteenth Century

George III had been on the throne since 1760

The price of wheat, barley and oats rose to record heights. Wheat fetched the previously unheard of price of nearly £6 a quarter. Food was scarce everywhere. Many people starved and flocked to obtain relief from the parish.

The cost of the war against France had made the country dependant on its own resources. The harvests were deficient but there was now more land under corn than there had been before 1790. This had been brought about by enclosing wastes and putting them into production. While this was advantageous to landowners; small farmers and cottagers lost grazing for their animals and could not survive.

The population of Dorking was 1,526 males, 1,532 females.

On 25th April 1800 "HENRY MARSH now of Thames Ditton did out of court surrender all that messuage ------- to JOHN TILT of the parish of Dorking, yeoman. Received from John Tilt £136 being the full consideration for any making the absolute surrender."

The unfortunate Henry Marsh could now pay his debt.

"I, John Stedman of the Parish of Dorking in the County of Surrey, Yeoman, do hereby acknowledge to have this day had and received of Henry Marsh late of Dorking aforesaid, Yeoman, but now of Thames Ditton in the said County all Principle and Interest Moneys due and owing to me whom or by virtue of a Conditional Surrender made to the use of me --------"

Henry Marsh returned to Holmwood the following year and a son was baptised in Dorking in 1801 (buried 1804)

JOHN TILT was the new copyholder. He was a yeoman who was gradually acquiring more and more property in the area. He came from the heavy clay country of Newdigate, had married a Dorking girl: Ann Peters, and they had four sons and four daughters.

John Tilt soon installed one of his sons, James, in the house. **JAMES TILT** had been married for eighteen months to Martha Randall. In their first august at Belchett Green Martha bore a daughter.

At this time a midwife's fee was 5 shillings, a bottle of brandy for the occasion was 2 shillings, and linen for the child cost 3 or 4 shillings.

To buy a coat in a shop was considered the height of extravagance. A foul-weather coat cost 13 shillings, a pair of shoes 7 shillings, a coarse linen shirt 4 shillings 6 pence, breeches 3 shillings 9 pence, a woman's common stuff gown 6 shillings 6 pence, cap 10 pence. A man earned about 7 shillings a week, with milk and small beer worth about 1 shilling. A woman earned a little by washing, keeping fowl, etc.

Dorking fowl were fattened on gruel made to special recipes. They often contained ground oats, sugar, hogs grease, pot liquor and milk. The gruel was fed to them for about two weeks before the fowls were sold, either to passing "higglers" or at the local markets.

SURREY WORDS.
cojer time = lunch time
trumpery = weeds
jag = cartload
plits = furrow slices
mow = straw stack
esh = stubble

In 1804 Napoleon Bonaparte became Emperor of France

"Quit roaring or Boney'll come and carry you off."

a frequent threat to children

During the time that John Tilt's sons had been growing into men he had taken on more and more land, but after the death of his wife in 1801 it would appear that he looked to the future less and less

He bought no more property and as time went on he began to reduce his holdings

---

Received this 3ʳᵈ day of October 1805 of Mʳ William Bellchamber the sum of One hundred and seventy pounds being the consideration of my having this day Surrendered ^a certain Customary Messuage lands and Hereditaments in the Parish of Dorking in the County of Surrey and parcel of the Manor of Dorking in the said County, I say received the same — me The mark of

£170

Witness —

Timy Hall —

X

John Tilt —

In 1805 John Tilt accepted an offer of £170 for the house at Betchett Green from William Betchamber, a cordwainer of the parish of Abinger. He already owned the other little house on the Green, known as "The Croft" which had been built by Mathew Marsh a few years before. Betchamber bought the property as an investment. He was a widower of middle years. His father had recently died, at the age of 85, and had left him some money.

"England expects that every man will do his duty"

21st October 1805.

There was a decisive victory in the BATTLE OF TRAFALGAR over the French. Sadly our Lord Nelson was killed, but Britain was freed from the threat of invasion. Napoleon went on to dominate Europe, and although he tried to weaken Britain he did not ruin her.

THE MOON

CRESCENT MOON ~ a moon in early stage of waxing

WANING (cusps or horns on the right)

WAXING (cusps or horns on the left)

FULL MOONS:

EASTER MOON ~ full moon after vernal equinox. i.e. when the Sun crosses the celestial equator in spring.

HONEY MOON ~ waxing full moon, deemed most propitious for marriage

HARVEST MOON ~ full moon occurring after autumn equinox (21st September)

HUNTER'S MOON ~ full moon in October after the harvest moon.

The tang of horse-radish said to be keenest at the full moon.

It is dangerous to sleep in moonlight

Spring wheat should be sown at the wane of the moon for a good crop.

It will be a wet month when there are two full moons in it.

The new moon brings a change of weather with it.

The Spring of 1806 was cold. William Belchamber sought a tenant for his new acquisition. He chose WILLIAM SMITH with his wife SARAH

Holmwood was little changed from earlier times. The Common itself was considered by strangers to be a wild and lawless tract of country across which they travelled hastily for fear of robbers.

The turnpike road carried traffic of all kinds. It was no novelty now for any Holmwood resident to see the passenger coaches which travelled regularly along it going to and from London.

As for the robbers that the travellers were afraid of, there were certainly desperate characters trudging the road. Usually the parish constables hustled them onwards in case they should become a burden on the Poor Rates. The local people had to contend with gypsies and with smugglers, who still operated despite the Napoleonic Wars. When a string of packhorses crossed the Common the local inhabitants acted deaf dumb and blind, and kept away from trouble.

People going to Horsham for a day at market found the town full of soldiers, most of them rough-spoken and drunken, from the barracks there, which had been built to train men to fight the French, and to repulse an invasion by Napoleon.

A COPY OF HIS SIGNATURE.

WILLIAM BELCHAMBER'S tenants, WILLIAM SMITH and his family were not destined for a long occupation of the house.

Belchamber decided to marry again, a spinster, Sarah Tovey, from his home-parish of Abinger. No doubt a new wife proved to be expensive, so he first sold "The Croft" on the other side of the Green for £90, and three years later he sold Betchett Green for £250, making a good profit on his investment of only five years before.

ABINGER — a long narrow parish, tranquil, with moss covered cottages, some isolated, tucked beside streams in the deep folds of the wooded hills.

Abinger Church

The new copyholder was GEORGE PANNELL, a Capel farmer. The bond "for quiet enjoyment of a Copyhold Estate in ye Manor of Dorking", to George Pannell was inscribed in the Court Rolls on 4th October 1810.

At Michaelmas William Smith and family moved out to one of John Tilt's cottages, and into the house went George Pannell's tenants: CAPTAIN MATHEW KENT, his wife VIRTUE and children RICHARD ROSCO and CECILIA

Judging by the Christian names of the new family in the house, the KENTS were not in the usual mould of a husbandman's or agricultural labourer's family such as those who had occupied it before. Just what kind of a Captain MATHEW KENT was has not been discovered. Perhaps he was down on his luck, or perhaps he wanted a simple country life. The Kents were probably objects of curiosity to the local inhabitants, and they would have been treated with suspicion.

It was becoming fashionable nowadays to observe the beauty of landscape, to notice the disposition of hills, trees and streams. "Picturesque" landscapes were sought out and noticed where they had been unremarked before.

MAY DAY ~ On 1st May children carried sticks decorated with flowers to sell to anyone with a coin to spare: "Please Ma'am remember the day, the first of May when I come round with my Maypole.

GOODING DAY ~ On the shortest day of the year, 21st December, old women went knocking on doors in the hope of receiving a coin.

1813 The eleventh Duke of Norfolk, who had recently enclosed and sold 720 acres of Horsham Common, ordered that the DORKING MARKET HALL, which housed prison cells, stocks, corn store-rooms, the firebell, etc., to be demolished, but he promised to build the town a new one. Unfortunately the Duke died and his executors refused to fund the building of a new market hall. The town never did have a new one.

The population of Dorking was about 3,000 of whom 1800 were on Poor Relief

1814 There was an exceptionally hard winter with the River Thames freezing over in February and a Frost Fair was held on it. Prices dropped due to an abundant harvest in 1813, so yeomen and farmers were badly off. Employment was scarce, both in town and countryside.

A period of DEPRESSION began. Relaxation of the POOR LAWS resulted resulted in large numbers drawing relief, while the income of those paying rates diminished, and they, too, became impoverished.

1815 AN IMPORTANT YEAR FOR ENGLAND

NAPOLEON was defeated in the BATTLE OF WATERLOO. He was sent away to the remote island of St. Helena. The war with France was over.

In Dorking there were celebrations. Crowds flocked into town, where, after dark, a candle burned in every window to give a festive air.

With the war over the home-coming soldiers and sailors swelled the masses of unemployed. One sixth of the adult population had been serving in the war, and the population of the country had increased by about one and three quarter million.

THE DEPRESSION WAS TO LAST FOR ABOUT A QUARTER OF A CENTURY

1815 marked the Kent's last year at the house. They left before Michaelmas. James Cooke then occupied it for a few months

GEORGE PANNELL, owner of the copyhold, died in early 1816. He had not made a will, and he left no live cattle with which to pay the Lord of the Manor a heriot.

It was not until 1820 that George Pannell's widow MARY sent her attorney to the Court Baron

When Pannell died the occupiers were Edward and Jane Vaughan, but they stayed for only two years.

"in the first year of the reign of our Sovereign Lord George the fourth."

MARY PANNELL was admitted tenant of the Lord of the Manor and she became the new copyholder on 22nd March 1820.

MICHAELMAS 1818 ~ the BUCKLAND FAMILY

Over the last twenty years the old house had seen many comings and goings, with no less than six families calling the place "home" during that time. The house was over two hundred years old and was probably in need of repairs.

The new occupier was JAMES BUCKLAND, 44 years old
       his wife was ELIZABETH
       his son was CHARLES , 7 years old.

In south-east England there were 60% of agricultural workers unemployed.

James, Elizabeth and Charles could have maintained themselves by growing all their own produce on the property and by using the Rights of Common on the Holmwood. (A house with Rights of Common was "a place with chances"). It is doubtful if, in the depressed times in which they lived, they could have made much by working for other people.

LEITH HILL FAIR 1819

Sunrise on Leith Hill

Everyone knew the landmark of Leith Hill Tower, on the highest point on the North Downs. The tower could no longer be climbed by its inner stair, for that had been blocked up, but there were panoramic views from the ridge where it stood. In 1819 a great fair was held there with booths, marquees, the Dorking town band and hundreds of people wearing their best clothes.

SPRING-HEELED JACK

No one knew who Spring-heeled Jack was or where he came from, but many people were afraid of meeting him. He was a macabre and dreadful figure who haunted lonely lanes and sprang up from behind hedges. To see him was enough to make a woman swoon in fright, and everyone knew someone who had an acquaintance who had seen him.

Elizabeth Buckland was expecting a baby, ten years after her only child Charles had been born. No doubt she was afraid that Spring-heeled Jack might pop up and cause a miscarriage. She was, however, spared, and in

✳ **SPRING 1821** her second son **JOHN BUCKLAND** was born.

He was baptised at St. Martin's, Dorking, on 17th June 1821

GHOSTS

It was in the interests of those concerned in smuggling to play upon the fears and superstitions of gullible people in order to deter them from roaming about at night. Thus stories of ghosts were rife. The wish hounds might run baying across the night sky to bring bad luck, or there might be a terrible phantom horseman, or a black calf foaming at the mouth and with eyes like lamps, or spectres without heads, and other frightening phenomena.

POACHING

Strong measures were taken to enforce the Game Laws. A poacher was often a hungry unemployed man with a large family. He might set snares on four or five nights a week in order to keep alive. Punishment was severe. There were spring guns and man traps hidden in estate woods which could severely maim. After 1817 a poacher, even if poaching without lights and unarmed, could be transported for seven years.

Many people were hungry. A "hummer supper" consisted of kidney fat from a ewe that had died, perhaps while lambing, fried with wild birds' eggs.

To take a bath was still considered dangerous to the health. Ordinary people did not undress between November and March for fear of catching a chill.

COACH TRAVEL

16 stage and mail coaches passed along the Holmwood turnpike road every day. The sound of the post horn as the coach approached the turnpike cottage near Beare Green would have been a familiar sound to little John Buckland.

The Horsham coach was the fastest. It could do the Horsham to London run, (38 miles) in 3½ hours, with several changes of horses. "The Comet", "The Accomodation", and "The Sovereign", regularly crossed Holmwood Common, travelling between London and Arundel, London and Worthing, London and Brighton.
The roads were often bad. Coaches were often overloaded with over 25 people and sometimes they overturned. There could be collisions, broken axles, runaway horses, a drunken coachman and many other mishaps.

FEBRUARY

The sunbeams on the hedges lie,
    The south wind murmers summer-soft;
The maids hang out white clothes to dry
    Around the elder-skirted croft:
A calm of pleasure listens round,
    And almost whispers winter by
While Fancy dreams of summer's sound
    And quiet rapture fills the eye.

                    John Clare 1793~1864

SMUGGLING

Although the war with France was over there were still taxes on many goods, and smuggling continued.

It is likely that James Buckland was involved with smugglers, for stories of it were passed down to his great grandson who later occupied the property.

Illicit luxuries that were transported by night by the smugglers had to be hidden by day. Perhaps James provided places to hide some of it, which was reputedly brought down a path from the Redlands hills to the rear of the house, from whence some may have been distributed further: perhaps to "The Nag's Head", midway across the Common, which was known as a haunt of smugglers.

Excise men and smugglers are rumoured to have had a skirmish on Betchett Green, where bullets were said to have scarred an oak tree there. Whether or not James was involved is not known.

Some contraband came from the Horsham direction, with some pack horse trains passing through Rusper, from there going to Newdigate and on along the eastern edge of the Holmwood where there was "The Bottle and Glass," a smugglers calling place.

Other loads would take a route through Capel, then uphill towards Anstiebury and Leith Hill, from there descending through thick woodland to Abinger and Wotton.

Overnight the contraband was occasionally hidden in holes and under bushes in the woods. It was said that if ever a man came across a cache of bundles and barrels hidden in some cave or barn the finder might make a mark on one of the packages and perhaps it would be left for him as payment for keeping quiet about the hiding place.

No doubt the young John Buckland imbibed with his milk tales of smuggling, wish hounds and headless horsemen.

FARM LABOURERS WERE DISSATISFIED, RESTLESS AND DESPERATE.

Steady work with a living wage was hard to find. While a family man in work might earn 9 shillings a week, many with regular jobs earned only 7 pence a day, which was less than a labourer had been able to earn nearly a hundred years before.

The labourers thought they should receive half a crown a day. (2s6d or 12½ new pence)

More and more landowners were investing in machines which not only did the farm work more quickly than men alone could do, but required less manpower. This gave the labouring man, who had been dissatisfied for years, a definite object on which to vent his feelings.

Even the most slow-witted labourer could understand that machines were now taking over the work that was rightfully his. When labourers were out of work they did not receive their meagre wages, nor did they receive the side benefits that came with employment, such as free beer, a stale pie or pudding, or, at threshing time, the chance to limp home with boots full of corn. Every grain helped, for planting, for flour, or just to feed the chickens.

The labourer focussed his hatred upon the machines, and often he did not appreciate that his unfortunate circumstances were as much due to the high prices of goods to buy, high rates, and several exceedingly wet seasons when some of the heavy clay soil of the area could not be worked and had to be abandoned.

1830-1831

No one ever actually met "Captain Swing". He was reputed to be the leader of the farm labourers, inciting them to make trouble for farmers and landowners. Threatening letters, signed by "Captain Swing" were often sent to farmers whose hay and straw ricks were subsequently set alight. The penalty for firing a rick was death, and for smashing a threshing machine it was transportation to Australia.

Ricks at nearby Trouts Farm were fired, while at Newdigate food was burned and machinery was smashed.

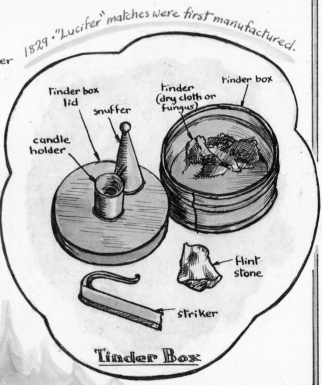

1829 "Lucifer" matches were first manufactured.

tinder box lid

snuffer

tinder (dry cloth or fungus)

tinder box

candle holder

flint stone

striker

Tinder Box

22nd November 1830.   Farm labourers from all over the district
flocked into Dorking for a meeting at The Red Lion.

Local magistrates were expected to give definite promises about
wages. Trouble from the mob of dissatisfied men was anticipated, and
the cavalry was in town to protect the magistrates. In Guildford there
was also a meeting and half the cavalry, about twenty-five, had gone
there to quell any disruption. Local tradesmen were pressed into service
as special constables, and they carried staves that had been sent
specially from the Home Office.

The magistrates kept the mob waiting for a very long time outside The Red Lion. The labourers grew angry and attacked the Inn
with stones, and with brooms grabbed from a passing donkey cart.

The cavalry came galloping up the main street and soon scattered
the rioters, flinging those they could catch into the coach house. Meanwhile one of the magistrates read the Riot Act from the top of the steps :

"Our sovereign Lord the king chargeth and commandeth all persons
being assembled immediately to disperse themselves and peaceably.
to repair to their habitations or to their lawful business...."

DESPITE "CAPTAIN SWING" AND THE PROTESTS OF THE FARM WORKERS
NOTHING WAS ACHIEVED. CONDITIONS WERE SLOW TO IMPROVE

1831 • Repeal of the GameLaws ~ the sale and purchase of game was legalised.
Eel pies were a delicacy of the time.
A bottled beer, called "shrub," which was a cordial of fruit juice and spirit was a popular drink.

1834 POOR LAW AMENDMENDMENT ACT

A generation of people had grown up which knew no source of income but Poor Relief. All those classed as paupers, (and they constituted a large section of the rural population), could, if able to work, apply to the parish. The parish would be obliged to hire them out at a low rate and subsidise their wages.

People who had saved money, or bought a cottage could not receive relief until they had lost everything and had become desperate paupers. If they hired themselves out for work they often could not command a fair wage because they could not compete with the low paid, subsidised, pauper.

After 1834 it became difficult for an able-bodied man to obtain relief unless he was actually admitted to the workhouse. No man wanted to lose his freedom and so he tried hard to find work. Only in sickness, or through accident, could a man now obtain out-relief from the parish.

The Amendment Act was an unpleasant remedy, especially to people who were poor through no fault of their own, but it resulted in the lazy and work-shy relying on their own resources.

A Central Authority was set up to direct administration and unite parishes. This resulted in Union Workhouses and the spreading of resources.

A SURREY SMOCK. Made of linen in off-white, beige and brownish colours, and sometimes oiled with linseed oil to keep out the wet.

1837

DAWN OF THE VICTORIAN ERA

During the opening years of the nineteenth century the kings: George III (1760-1820), George IV (1820-1830) and William IV (1830-1837), had not affected the running of the country. This had been conducted by Parliament.

In 1837 the young Queen Victoria came to the throne

In that year there was a serious epidemic of influenza in Dorking with people in every family affected.

The Duke of Norfolk sold 120 acres of Holmwood Common to Mr. and Mrs. Francis Larpent. They built a fine house – the first gentleman's residence in the district. People with money, who lived in large country mansions, and who earned their money from business in London, were a new phenomenon. Previously local people had made a living from the land where they lived and each filled his niche in the order of country life. There had been no greatly marked divisions between upper and lower classes, but this was changing.

A NEW CHURCH Mrs. Charlotte Larpent was the first of her kind in the area. Once settled in her new house, she, with her mother and the owner of Kitlands set about having a church built for the local inhabitants. IT WAS COMPLETED IN 1838, COST £1,000, AND THE VICAR WAS REV. J. UTTERTON

MR. BUCKLAND and the HORSE THIEVES.

Many horses were left out all night on the Common and they made fine pickings for horse thieves. Gipsies were frequently the culprits.

A Dorking man, Charles Rose, writing in 1876, recalled that in about 1838, two gypsies had been seen viewing the horses on the Common. Thus alerted several Holmwood men banded together to try to catch them in the act. They kept watch on the byroads leading from the Common, and eventually two gipsies mounted on stolen horses appeared.

They were caught by Messrs. Buckland and Sims, said to be the strongest of the watchers, with others running to help.

From 1837 the Death Penalty was no longer enforced for stealing.

N.B. Whether the Buckland concerned was father James, age 64, son Charles, age 28, or son John, age 18, or more than one of them, is not recorded, but it was almost certainly this family.

A PERIOD OF DEPRESSION

Poor people were thankful for any kind of food. In some houses bread was rationed; the boys being allowed a larger portion than the girls. Labourers could not afford enough bread on their small wages. Corn was dear because its importation from abroad was restricted.

There was a fashion for establishing schools, and Holmwood's benefactress, Mrs. Larpent established a school in South Lodge, a house within her parkland. Joseph Dolman and his wife Elizabeth were engaged as teachers. Many parents could not afford the few pennies required to have their children taught. Others were suspicious of book learning. Many educated people thought schooling would spoil labouring people and make them dissatisfied.

The First School

Elizabeth taught the girls in a downstairs room. Joseph taught the boys in a hut.

In 1841 James Tilt, who had once occupied Betchett Green, still lived on the Holmwood. He was aged 75; Martha was 70; and their son Peter, an agricultural worker, aged 30, lived with them.

Edward Vaughan, another who occupied the house briefly, died in 1841 in Dorking, age 73.

102

BEARE GREEN PROSECUTING SOCIETY

Farmers in the vicinity of Beare Green, at the south-west corner of the Holmwood, formed a Prosecuting Society in June 1779. The members each paid a subscription from which fund fees were paid for information, expenses, etc., towards catching thieves and murderers.

In 1839 a £2.00 Reward was paid to Mr. Adds when Thomas Amey, James Constable, George Bivard and Henry Attree were convicted of stealing Mr. Wood's fat geese from an outhouse. £23.1s was paid for the prosecution. Henry Attree turned Queen's evidence, the others were transported.

In 1841 2s. 6d was paid to "Hue and Cry" for advertisement after the loss of a horse belonging to Mr. Charman (of Breakspeares Farm).

In 1842 Henry and George Harden of Newdigate were caught stealing wood from a hedgerow on Mr. Henry Nash's farm at Newdigate. The Committee met specially, and recommended that the boys be taken before a magistrate and reprimanded. This was afterwards done.

A man was sentanced for 3 months for receiving a fowl stolen by his son, who decamped, and another 6 months hard labour for stealing some geese

There were no local policemen, although in London a Metropolitan Police Force had been formed in 1829, following Sir Robert Peel's "Peelers" of 1820

At about this time many people left the countryside and flocked to towns to work for long hours in factories, which were being set up for the manufacture of all kinds of things————.

Men living on the Holmwood were occupied as lath-cleavers, hoop-shavers, sawyers, carpenters, bricklayers, braziers, shoemakers, etc.

In 1842 Mary Pannell, the copyhold owner of Betchett Green, died. Her son Charles Pannell, who resided in Chelsea, was admitted as the new copyholder on 6 December 1843

Charles Pannell

a copy of his signature.

THE BUCKLAND FAMILY

In about 1845 JOHN Buckland married HANNAH KING.

On 9th August 1846 their daughter MARY ANN was christened in the little Holmwood church that had been built eight years before——?.

It seems likely that JOHN and HANNAH lived with JOHN's parents at Betchett Green. It may have been at this time that the house was divided and a second stairway made so that the young couple and their baby could have two tiny rooms downstairs and a bedroom above to themselves.

The following dry cold winter was an unhappy one for the Bucklands. First old JAMES BUCKLAND died, age 72, in November 1846, and four months later the baby, MARY ANN, died.

Old Surrey Speech

buzzly – short and plump

peter-grievious – fretful

gooning – stupid

doddish – infirm in mind and body

beayled – tired out.

mould – garden soil

"a little masterpiece – a clever child

"nothing but a frame" – emaciated person.

the flies "tarrify" – the flies worry.

boffle – confusion

"shut (or shet)" a horse into the shafts of a cart – put him in

"agen" the gate – near

ground to grow "sauce" in – vegetables

a bit "leary" – faint from want of food

winter pickets – sloes

a "bush" – a thorn (i.e. in the foot)

• 1845. The Irish Potato Crop failed, causing thousands of Irish to die of starvation and thousands more to leave Ireland. As an emergency measure foreign grain was permitted to be imported.

• 1846. The Corn Laws were repealed, giving little restriction on the importation of corn from abroad. As a consequence bread became cheaper.

COSTS FROM THE HOME ECONOMIST MAGAZINE 1848 :–

A good cotton dress	7s 8d	A common working-gown	3s 6d
A pair of stockings	2s 0d	A pair of shoes	4s 0d
A shawl	12s 0d	A petticoat	2s 0d

It was believed that flannel should be worn next to the skin and that many deaths from cholera might have been prevented by this.

In 1849 two thirds of the men who married were unable to write their names, while half of their brides could not write.

In 1850 wheat stood at 40s 3d a quarter, a low price after a good harvest the year before.
The Mill on the Holmwood was owned by Joseph Killick.

There were two common ways of measuring dry goods :–

"Strike measure", used for corn, peas, beans, etc., where the container was stricken level with the top edge.

"Heaped measure", used for potatoes, apples and large fruit, etc. which had spaces between them where the fruit was piled up above the top edge.

THE BUCKLAND FAMILY • The year after Mary Ann died John and Hannah had a son, Alfred, and then in 1850 John (called Jack). Both boys lived. In 1851, when the Census was taken John's old widowed mother, Elizabeth, was not at home. John was a labourer, aged 29, and his wife Hannah was 25 years old.

Over the hill to the poor-house — my childr'n dear, goodbye!
Many a night I've watched you when only God was nigh;
And God will judge between us; but I will always pray
That you shall never suffer the half I do today.

Will Carleton   1891

•1852• July was very hot with several people succumbing to sunstroke while they were working in the fields. At Newdigate John Hayter died of sunstroke, as did Stephen Longhurst, aged 45, after haymaking at Bonnets Farm, Capel.

At the end of the year there were severe outbreaks of foot and mouth disease.

•1854• THE CRIMEAN WAR began after 40 years of almost unbroken peace. Russia sought an outlet to the Mediterranean by gaining control of the Balkan Peninsula and it also wanted to add India to the Russian Empire.

Britain, France and Turkey sent armies to the Crimean Peninsula in southern Russia. After great hardship the fortress of Sebastopol was captured.

• THE BUCKLAND FAMILY •

John and Hannah Buckland had a third son, Isaac, who was baptised in May 1854, but he died at age two years.

At the end of January 1859 old Elizabeth Buckland died in the Dorking Union Workhouse. The funeral was at Holmwood on 2nd February.

By this time John and Hannah were expecting their last child. This time it was a girl, baptised on 14th June 1859. She was called HANNAH after her mother, and lived a long life———'.

The Bucklands took in a lodger: a working man. He was a middle-aged man by the name of David Briggs, from Warnham just over the Surrey/Sussex border. He was a lath-cleaver and was employed, no doubt, in nearby Holmwood woods.

farming Women worked in the fields at clod-breaking, hoeing, haymaking, harvesting, etc. in season.
Nowadays scythes were used in preference to the old reaping hook with serrated cutting edge. A team of five, with a scyther, gatherer, binder, stooker and raker could harvest a steady two acres a day. In the old days with a reaping hook it took a man three days to cut an acre of wheat.
Machines to help with farm work were fast being invented and coming into use, such as a steam engine to drive a plough.

from a water-colour, about 1860,

by Miss Wickert the vicar's daughter,

showing the stream at the back of the house with the roofs of Wiggons in the dip beyond Betchett Green and the church, now with a tower, on the hill beyond.

Victorian Values

People believed they should be frugal and thrifty, and that the secret of success was to be industrious; to be willing to work hard, and to persevere.

Piety and religious observance were greatly to be encouraged, also temperance, punctuality and not wasting time.

The Devil finds mischief for idle hands.

Where there's a will there's a way.

Take care of the pence and the pounds will take care of themselves.

Marriage without means is like a horse without beans.

There was a great gulf between the classes. A man's social status was determined by the kind of work he did, and there was a strong dividing line between manual and non-manual workers.

"God bless the squire and his relations
And keep us in our proper stations."

"We want no aid of barricade to show a front to Wrong;
We have a citadel in Truth, more durable and strong:
Calm words, great thoughts, unflinching Faith have never striven in vain;
They've won our battles many a time — and so they shall again."
from "British Freedom" by C. Mackay.

After Prime Minister Lord Palmerston died in 1865, William Ewart Gladstone and Benjamin Disraeli were the succeeding Prime Ministers. They introduced many reforms to improve the lot of the people, but wealth remained unevenly distributed.

The mill had 32 ft. patent wind sails and two pairs of stones. It was a post mill.

The mill house had four bedrooms, dairy, oven, shop, granary, stabling, piggeries, etc.

Holmwood Windmill about 1860   From a sketch by Miss E. Wickert.

HOLMWOOD was becoming quite a popular place

for town people to visit in the carriages in the summer. They
liked to take the country air and to look at the pretty
scenery. Several cottages accommodated visitors, who could also
lodge at the "Holly and Laurel" inn.

In the mid-1850's Baron Larpent, with a committee,
appointed a Ranger for the Duke of Norfolk to look after the
Common. His job was to prevent thieving, including catching people
who cut holly or took greenwood that they were not entitled to.
There was now a policeman, Mr. Page, who prosecuted those caught.

Besides the Larpents and the Heaths, other gentry were
coming into the area. Some bought the dilapidated squatters'
cottages on the Common, knocked them down and built fine
brick houses. Mr. Leopold Heath occupied Moorhurst, which
had been converted from a small farmhouse into a large
residence. He set about building a great new house, Anstie Grange,
higher up the hill from Moorhurst, towards ancient Anstiebury Camp.

School

By the mid-1860's many of the local children attended school; young Hannah Buckland amongst them. A fee was charged and school was not compulsory until 1876. Even then the Act was not always enforced. In general, more than half the pupils that went to school attended for less than 100 days a year, and most went for only a year or two and left before they were twelve. There were frequent days off for the children to do tasks at home and traditional seasonal work on farms.

On May 1st they were away carrying flower-bedecked poles and garlands round the district. In June at Holmwood they picked cherries and whortleberries. Then there came the Friendly Societies' club holidays and the Annual Treat at the Vicarage. There was hay-making and harvest, and, in October, gathering acorns for pigs. Quite often the school was closed for epidemics of measles or scarlet fever.

A new building for a school had been built in Holmwood in 1844

Holmwood School

"The spirits of your fathers
Shall start from every wave!
For the deck it was their field of Fame,
And Ocean was their grave:
Where Blake and mighty Nelson fell
Your manly hearts shall glow,
As ye sweep through the deep
While the stormy tempests blow;
While the battle rages long and loud,
And the stormy tempests blow."

from Ye Mariners of England,
by Thomas Campbell.

"The meteor-flag of England
Shall yet terrific burn,
Till danger's troubled night depart
And the star of peace return....."

RAILWAYS

By 1848 there were 5,000 miles of railways constructed over the whole country, but it was not until 1867 that the trains came to Holmwood, and a station opened at Beare Green.

Local people walked to see the navvies building the line, taking eggs, apples, strawberries, cherries, etc. to sell to the men and their followers.

The navvies' work was hard and dangerous. They were rough, strong, and fearsome men, with a reputation for drunken fighting and for terrorising the neighbourhood after pay day. They moved across country as the line was laid.

At Holmwood the navvies lived in huts. Some had families with them and the children were given lessons. In the evenings classes were held for the men.

After the station was opened the station master's uniform was a frock-coat and top hat, while the porters wore white jackets.

TRAVEL BY TRAIN SOON SUPERCEDED LONG-DISTANCE JOURNEYS BY HORSE-DRAWN COACH, AND COACHES WERE SEEN ON THE ROADS LESS AND LESS FREQUENTLY.

Between 1866 and 1874 the numbers of cattle and sheep in Great Britain greatly increased. An Act of 1866 made the slaughter of diseased animals compulsory and by 1871 rinderpest was eradicated.

In the mid-1870's barbed wire began to make it's appearance

From about 1874, for about 20 years, there was a depression in the countryside, owing to bad seasons, with poor harvests, low prices and losses of livestock. In the south, south-west and south-east of England conditions for farm workers were very bad while many farmers went out of business. The harvest of 1879 was the worst of the century.

• THE BUCKLAND FAMILY • In 1873 John Buckland died at the age of 52, leaving his wife Hannah with nearly half her life still to live.

His sons Alf and Jack were aged 25 and 23 years old, and his daughter Hannah was 14. Alf had been married for three years to Victoria Stanford from Warnham and they both lived with the rest of the family for a time before moving to a gamekeeper's cottage at Wotton.

9 July 1874 — Charles Pannell, of 47 Nutfield Rd. East Dulwich, in the County of Surrey, Gentleman, surrendered the copyhold of the old house for the sum of £555. The Pannell family had owned it for 64 years.

The buyer was Major Rhode Hawkins, Esquire.

Mr. Major Rhode Hawkins was an architect employed by the Education Department, and he had built himself a large red brick mansion, "Redlands," on the edge of the woods. On the northern side of Holmwood Common a village was growing up and Mr. Hawkins was the architect for the new church there. S. John the Evangelist was built in 1875.

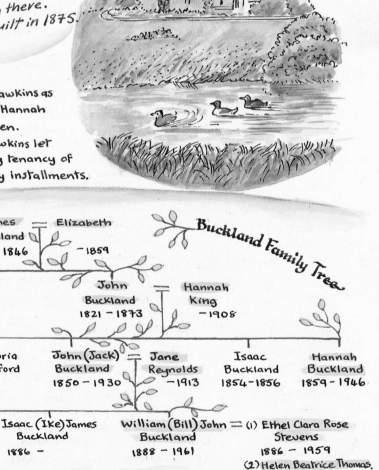

Jack worked for Mr. Hawkins as a woodman and his sister Hannah worked in the Redlands kitchen. From Christmas Day 1874 Mr. Hawkins let the old house to Jack on a yearly tenancy of £10 a year, payable in quarterly installments.

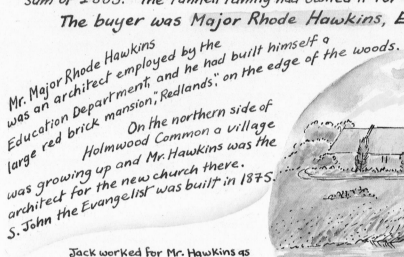

Buckland Family Tree

James Buckland 1774–1846 = Elizabeth –1859

Charles Buckland 1811–

John Buckland 1821–1873 = Hannah King –1908

Mary Ann Buckland 1846 3 months

Alfred Buckland 1848– = Victoria Stanford

John (Jack) Buckland 1850–1930 = Jane Reynolds –1913

Isaac Buckland 1854–1856

Hannah Buckland 1859–1946

John Buckland 1883 7 months

Charles Henry Buckland 1885–

Isaac (Ike) James Buckland 1886–

William (Bill) John Buckland 1888–1961

John = (1) Ethel Clara Rose Stevens 1886–1959
(2) Helen Beatrice Thomas.

112

The Fly Proprietor and Greengrocer.

At Holmwood Railway Station one of the porters was a young man who came from Steyning in Sussex. His name was John William Hoad. Working as a porter he could see the need for a form of transport to carry passengers and their luggage between the station and their destinations.

Jack Buckland left his employment with Mr. Hawkins and he and Hoad set up together in a cab hire business. The partnership did not survive for long and the two men went their separate ways, each giving a similar service.

John Hoad expanded, did removals and became a carrier, travelling twice weekly between London and Ockley. This he continued for nearly sixty years.

Meanwhile Jack continued with his cab (or "Fly"), he sold green-grocery, even travelled round on horse-back selling gin and any-thing else where he could make a penny or two.

Jack also courted and married a girl by the name of JANE REYNOLDS.

1880's Experiments to construct a "horseless" carriage were under way in various parts of Europe and U.S.A. Development of the internal combustion engine began.

In mid-January 1881 the worst snowstorm of the 19th century occurred. Immense snowdrifts brought everything to a standstill and caused the deaths of many animals and of some people.

THE BUCKLAND FAMILY

JACK BUCKLAND and his wife JANE at first lived at the old house with Jack's mother and his sister. Their first child, John, was born in 1883 but died 7 months later. It was thought that the baby's death affected Jane's mind because she suffered bouts of mental illness afterwards.

In 1884 their landlord Major Rhode Hawkins died, age 63, and it was some time before his will and property were sorted out.

Jack and Jane's second child was Charles Henry, born in May 1885. That year there was a summer drought and a shortage of root crops. Charles lived, and so did their later children: Isaac James, or Ike, born 1886 and WILLIAM JOHN, or BILL, born in 1888.

By this time Jack and Jane had moved to a new house in the village which was growing up a quarter of a mile away, near the turnpike road. In 1885 a horse-drawn bus had begun a regular service, running the three miles between Holmwood and Dorking.

Had the turnpike road passed a little nearer to Betchett Green no doubt the ancient Green would have become the centre point for the village, but it was left apart with modern life passing it by.

20th JUNE 1887 · QUEEN VICTORIA'S GOLDEN JUBILEE · A great festive day in fine weather. Everywhere the people rejoiced. The Holmwood people flocked to the sports at the "Holly and Laurel", and to see the bonfire and fireworks. In Dorking there were flags, processions, feasts, fireworks, etc.

God Save the Queen

The Pig: Most cottagers kept a pig if they could possibly afford to buy a weaner in the first place. Children collected acorns, sow thistles, dandelions, to supplement the pig's food. Everyone watched it grow and commented on it.

When it was ready for killing a pig sticker was usually engaged to slaughter it.

It was thought that if it were killed when the moon was waning the bacon would shrink in the cooking. No pregnant or menstruating woman could touch the meat or it would spoil.

The Friendly Societies

One of the oldest Friendly Societies in the district originated in 1799 at the "Surrey Yeoman" in Dorking. The growth in the number of Societies continued through the 19th century. They raised funds which were used by their members in times of need, such as for insurance against fire or loss, or for maintenance during unemployment, or funeral expenses. Funds were used too for social gatherings.

The members were usually skilled workmen who could afford the subscription. The idea was for people to save for a rainy day, in the Victorian tradition of thrift and self-help.

The Ockley Society attracted members from far and wide, and on its club day there was a grand fair on the green for everyone. At Holmwood there was a Society at "The Norfolk Arms", and another, "Pledges", at the "Holly and Laurel". The landlord's name was Pledge. This fair, held annually on the second Tuesday in July, was a big event, with fairground, circus, dancing on the cricket green to the Dorking Town Band, for everyone, members or not, until midnight.

The large Societies began to take over, and by the end of the century the Foresters met at "The Norfolk Arms", with most local subscribers belonging to it. The Foresters combined with the Oddfellows for the annual parade and fair.

At the beginning of the 1890's the Holmwood windmill was demolished. A new Victorian house had already been built on the site of the old Mill House.

In September 1891, the school opened free of charge. At Holmwood about 50 children opted to pay their former fees into the Post Office Savings Bank.

In 1892 a SHOP HOURS ACT was passed limiting a week's work to 74 hours for anyone under eighteen years old.

In March 1891 severe blizzards devastated many orchards and woods. The winter of 1894/95 brought prolonged freezing weather, making farm work impossible and money short.

"Wiggons"

Drawn from a photograph. 1890's.

22nd June 1897. The country celebrated QUEEN VICTORIA'S DIAMOND JUBILEE in brilliant weather. At Holmwood there was tea at the "Holly and Laurel" with every child being given a commemorative mug, and there were sports, fireworks and a bonfire.

116

THE BUCKLAND FAMILY • Jack Buckland lived in the village, but he was frequently at the old house where he grew vegetables to sell in his shop. He rented a field opposite "Wiggons", where he had stables and sheds for his vehicles, and he kept his horses either in the field or grazing out on the Common.

His mother, Hannah, and sister, Hannah, both lived at the old house, his sister going out daily to do domestic work.

Jack's wife Jane became more and more prone to bouts of mental illness, and was obliged to spend longer and longer periods of time in the asylum at Haywards Heath in Sussex. As a consequence the two Hannahs took over the rearing of Jack's boys: Charlie, Ike, and little Bill. They cared for Bill almost from babyhood, as Jane was confined to the asylum shortly after his birth, and did not come home again.

1899

Several local men went to fight in the Boer War. The Dutch settlers of the Transvaal and Orange Free State declared war on Britain. They did not want British interference, and influxes of British gold prospectors.

> There groups of merry children played;
> There youths and maidens dreaming strayed;
> O precious hours! O golden prime
> And affluence of love and time!
> Even as a miser counts his gold,
> Those hours the ancient timepiece told~
>   "For ever~ never!
>   Never~ for ever!"
>
> Henry Wadsworth Longfellow. 1807-1882

In 1900 Holmwood acquired it's first district nurse. The villagers had previously paid a subscription to an Association and one of the nurses employed by this was brought from Capel by carriage or cart when she was needed. The annual subscription for the nurse's services was 1 shilling for artisans, 1s 6d for outdoor servants and 2s. for farmers. For each visit they were charged 1d, 2d and 6d respectively. The nurse informed the wealthy ladies of the parish about particular cases of hardship and sickness so that they could visit and perhaps take along nourishing food.

"THE NEW WOMAN" A more liberated woman began to emerge. With the growing popularity of bicycling women could travel independently, and there were more opportunities to work outside the home in capacities other than as servants.

FERN CUTTING · Notices announcing the start of Fern Cutting on the Common were posted in the village in August.

On the last Monday of the month those living in houses with Rights of Common had to cut around the patch of bracken they wished to claim. The claim areas were traditional and there were rarely disagreements. The patch for the old house lay on the east side of the turnpike road opposite the church. After a path round the bracken had been cut the patch could be left until September or October. Cutting it was hard work as it was usually tangled with brambles. It was cut one day, carried the next, and then stacked, to be used throughout the winter for animals' bedding.

22nd JANUARY 1901 · Queen Victoria died at Osborne House on the Isle of Wight. Mourning was International.
"The Queen is gone from her people, full of years and honour."

118

In 1901 Marconi made the first transatlantic radio signals from Poldhu in Cornwall, to Signal Hill in Newfoundland.

26th JUNE 1902 • Festivities for the Coronation of King Edward.
The lighting of the bonfire at Holmwood was delayed for a few days as the new king was unwell, but other celebrations took place.

1902• In the summer the soldiers came home from the Boer War. Three local men had won distinctions, and Major Heath had rendered efficient service with his hot-air balloon when they were besieged at Ladysmith. Before the war the Major had frequently flown his balloon over the Holmwood area, and the people had become accustomed to it.

Shrove Tuesday Football.
Annual football matches in town streets had been held in Britain at least from the 15th century. Dorking too had its match.
After a procession, with musicians and a standard borne aloft bearing two coloured footballs, the game began at the church gates at about 1 p.m.
It was a rough and violent game, often with damage to property and participants. In earlier times the game
"Kick away both Whig and Tory, Wind and water Dorking's Glory."
had included duckings in the brook and floundering for the ball in slaughterhouse waste. The first Dorking match was probably held in the early 1800's ～ The last match held in Dorking took place in 1906.

Dorking High Street

Jack's boys were growing into men. The oldest boy Charlie, worked with his father in the village. Ike had a wild nature. He joined the Navy but did not stay in it for long; later he went travelling like a gypsy.

Bill lived with his grandmother and Aunt Hannah. He was a lively boy, a "card". He had a fine voice and sang regularly in the church choir.

In April 1908 old Hannah Buckland died, aged 82. By this time Bill was employed as a houseboy at Anstie Grange, the home of Cuthbert Heath. The Grange had been built in 1862.

The Heath family had been in the area since the early 1800's, and had been associated with such properties as Kitlands and Moorhurst.

Cuthbert Heath was a charming gentleman who had started his working life in an insurer's office, and he went on to become the founder of the firm Lloyd's of London.

Bill's Aunt Hannah was now left on her own in the old house, although Jack and the boys were frequent callers. She let out half of the house to another single woman, a Miss Fishlock, who spent much of her time executing beautiful needlework.

Hannah Buckland

A COPY OF HER SIGNATURE.

1908 • The Old Age Pensions Bill was passed. It granted a weekly payment of five shillings to men and women over seventy years of age.

Recipe for Sloe Gin

Fill a screw topped jar with alternate layers of pricked **Sloes** and **Sugar**. Leave until Sugar is dissolved. Add **Gin** to cover all the fruit, leaving a space at the top of the jar.
            Keep in the dark for three months, shaking the jar well twice a week. Strain through flannel, bottle and cork.

1911 was a scorching hot summer, with water scarce and the wood and fields so parched that a spark could have set them alight.

Holmwood now had its own horse-drawn FIRE ENGINE, a second hand machine bought for £60 plus £32 for pipes and a hooter which called the volunteers from their regular work. The engine had been bought from collections made in the village after Bregsells Farm burned down and people had been upset by the cries of the animals trapped in the buildings.

Up on the turn-pike road, in a fine new house, lived Mr. Pethick Lawrence. He was the first man locally to own a motor car, and he was a sympathiser with the Suffragette movement. Several Suffragette ladies came to his house to rest after their ordeals in prison. He built another house nearby for a holiday home for single mothers from London.

NATIONAL INSURANCE ACT gave free medical treatment for working people and an allowance of money when they were ill or were out of work through no fault of their own. At this time FARMING was sound and prosperous. Most farmers in England and Wales were tenant farmers on estates. Market-gardening and fruit growing prospered too. Labour saving machines and new strains of seed made their appearance and methods improved. Even so, much food was imported.

On 13th September 1913 Jack's wife JANE BUCKLAND was buried at Holmwood. She had died, age 55, in the asylum at Haywards Heath

The heirs of Mr. Major Rhode-Hawkins decided to sell Betchett Green by auction at The King's Head Hotel, at Horsham on 2nd September 1914.

THE VERY
DESIRABLE SMALL PROPERTY
(COPYHOLD)

It was described as an old-fashioned brick and half-timbered cottage, roofed with tiles, charmingly placed on the outskirts of Holmwood Common, with a productive garden well stocked with fruit trees. It had three bedrooms, two sitting rooms, a wash house with a copper, a scullery with stone sink, bread-oven and copper, and outside was a detached timber-built earth closet. The water supply was laid on from Redlands estate to a large galvanised iron tank.

The property was "let on a yearly tenancy to Miss Buckland, an excellent tenant of old standing, at the moderate rent of £10 per annum. Land Tax about 3s 11½d. Tithe 3s. 4d.

The auction never took place

In 1914 plans made by many people did not come to fruition. On 2nd August Belgium was invaded by Germany. On 4th August BRITAIN declared war on GERMANY.

The Great War had begun.

At the end of August thousands of Belgian refugees began to arrive in Britain. Some of them came to Holmwood.

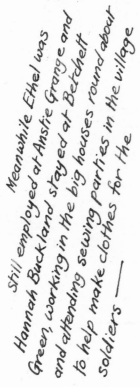

BILL BUCKLAND was now a footman at Anstie Grange. He was courting a cook who worked there too. She was ETHEL CLARA ROSE STEVENS, two years older than Bill.

While Bill was outgoing and ebullient, Ethel was quiet and shy. Bill was a country boy and Ethel a town girl who declared she disliked the country. She was the oldest of nine children and had been born in Fulham.

ENLIST NOW
RALLY ROUND THE FLAG
YOUR COUNTRY NEEDS YOU

The war was seen as a fight of British Good, against German Evil: the lion against the eagle.

Men queued to volunteer for the fighting. Those who went from Holmwood received a fatherly talk from Cuthbert Heath in his study at Anstie Grange.

On 9th November 1914 Bill Buckland enlisted at Horsham in the 4th Battalion of the Royal Sussex Regiment.

Meanwhile Ethel was still employed at Anstie Grange and Hannah Buckland stayed at Betchett Green, working in the big houses round about and attending sewing parties in the village to help make clothes for the soldiers ————

Anstie Grange

123

"Do Your Bit" and "Carry On" were the catch phrases of the time. People were proud to have a "Khaki Hero" in their family.

Besides men, most fit horses, unless they were mares in foal, were requisitioned for war. In every parish horses were bought, the farmers being compelled to part with them. None could be hidden away. People were very saddened to see the horses go.

At Holmwood the oak and chestnut trees on the Redlands hills were felled to make pit props and line trenches.

On 17th July 1915 BILL BUCKLAND embarked with his regiment for the GALLIPOLI Peninsular in Turkey, where war had been raging since the end of April. They landed at Suvla Bay and were sent to fill a gap in the firing line. It was Bill's first real taste of fighting. The British ran out of men and out of water, but Bill survived. At the end of the year the British left Suvla Bay.

If I should die, think only this of me
That there's some corner of a foreign field
That is forever England. There shall be
In that rich earth a richer dust concealed;
A dust whom England bore, shaped, made aware,
Gave, once, her flowers to love, her ways to roam,
A body of England's, breathing English air,
Washed by the rivers, blest by suns of home.....

by Rupert Brooke.
1887 - 1915

The Germans began Zeppelin raids on Britain, dropping bombs from the huge airships on East Anglia, then on London.

Bill Buckland and Ethel Stevens ≈ drawn from a photograph ≈

IN THE SPRING OF 1916 BILL BUCKLAND AND ETHEL STEVENS WERE MARRIED IN DORKING.

Thousands of soldiers were slaughtered in France in the Battle of the Somme on 1st July 1916. The fighting there continued until November. With the long lists of dead and wounded being printed in the newspapers the government could no longer present to the people a picture of war as splendid and heroic.

Compulsory conscription was introduced and all fit men between the ages of 18 and 41 were called up to war.

Women worked at all kinds of jobs that had previously been barred to them: in munitions factories, as "conductorettes" on buses, as land girls doing heavy tasks on farms, etc.

AT HOLMWOOD Hannah Buckland took in two of Ethel's nephews who were motherless, and who, living in London were in danger from German bombing raids.

In September 1916 Cuthbert Heath gave Anstie Grange to the War Office for use as a hospital for officers and he himself paid for the house to be fitted out. Motor lorries ferried wounded men from the railway station to Anstie Grange, crossing Betchett Green on the way. Meanwhile Ethel stayed on to cook for the wounded men, and Cuthbert Heath's daughter, Genesta, worked as a pantry maid.

By 1917 Government Departments were regulating the lives of ordinary people. Rules came into force forbidding such things as bonfires, buying binoculars, trespassing on allotments, giving bread to any dog, poultry or horse, etc.

Fighting in France and Flanders continued with nightmare casualties in seas of mud:

"Far, far from Ypres I long to be
Where German snipers can't pot at me.
Think of me crouching where the worms creep
Waiting for something to put me to sleep."
Soldier's Lullaby.

By **1918** an extra three-million acres of land had been put under cultivation. The Women's Land Army, conscientious objectors, prisoners of war, soldiers, children, and men who were too old or unfit to fight, worked on the land.

In mid-1918 the conscription age was raised to 51.

and women over the age of 30 were permitted to vote in municipal elections.

Daily life became increasingly difficult and miserable, there were restrictions, shortages and disillusionment.

Between June 1918 and May 1919 influenza killed 150,000 people.

On 11th November 1918 church bells rang out everywhere

~ The Great War was over ~

The Germans were beaten, there were wild celebrations, but 745,000 British soldiers were killed, one and a half million wounded, and 500,000 horses dead.

BILL BUCKLAND miraculously escaped being wounded until shortly before the Armistice, when he was so severely wounded in the right leg that it had to be amputated.

He was discharged from the Army on 31st May 1919, at the age of 31. He was awarded the British War Medal, Victory Medal and the 1914-15 Star.

Bill undertook a training scheme for disabled servicemen, learning boot and shoe repairing.

He returned home on crutches to his aunt Hannah and to his wife Ethel.

THE 1920's

The war had changed England.
The old ways of life had been shaken to their foundations.
Womens' lives in particular were more liberated. Women wore short skirts, dispensed with chaperons, smoked in public.

Men coming home from the war, especially those who were disabled, found it difficult to obtain work. Many were poverty stricken and reduced to selling boxes of matches in the streets, singing for pennies, or begging.

Britain was entering a severe depression, where work, money and self-esteem were difficult to come by, and the cost of living rose.

TIME PASSETH AWAY LIKE A SHADOW

CARPE · DIEM

21 May 1920. Bill Buckland and his aunt Hannah Buckland bought Betchett Green for £300 from the heirs to Mr. Hawkins' estate AFTER 100 YEARS OF OCCUPATION BY THE BUCKLAND FAMILY IT FINALLY BELONGED TO THEM.

Hannah occupied the larger portion of the house, where Jack, Bill's father, often stayed too. Bill and Ethel lived in two tiny rooms down-stairs, and the bedroom above them.

With his land, the Common, a hard working wife and aunt, Bill managed. He had 2 horses, 2 cows and some pigs.

❧FARMING❧

The government withdrew help it had given to farmers to increase production during the war. As a result farmers struggled along with hardly any income and were unable to pay their workers a living wage.

In 1922 designated grades of milk were introduced, with segregated herds of cattle being tested for bovine tuberculosis. Their milk was bottled and labelled "Certified Milk". This was the beginning of the withdrawal of herds from commons, as certified cows could not mix with others who might carry the disease.

Increasing efforts were being made to cope with diseases of livestock. In 1922, 1923 and 1924, there were severe outbreaks of foot and mouth disease, which cost the country 3 million pounds in compensation for slaughtered beasts.

After the war farms specialising in poultry sprang up, and schemes for the distribution of day-old chicks and eggs put into operation. A National Mark was adopted for eggs.

In Dorking, on 1st March 1926, the market was moved from the main street to a nearby site behind the shops. Congestion in the street had become intolerable as the market was large and included cattle pens. ———

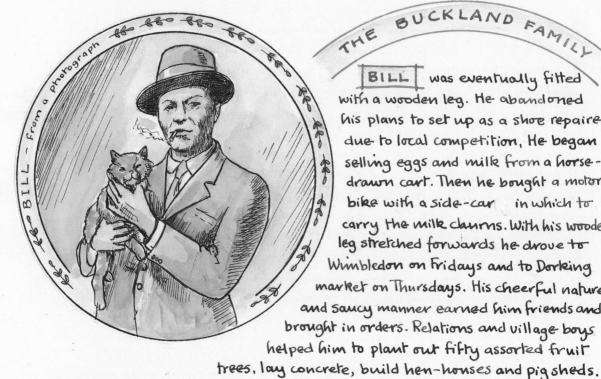

BILL – from a photograph

THE BUCKLAND FAMILY

[BILL] was eventually fitted with a wooden leg. He abandoned his plans to set up as a shoe repairer, due to local competition. He began selling eggs and milk from a horse-drawn cart. Then he bought a motor-bike with a side-car in which to carry the milk churns. With his wooden leg stretched forwards he drove to Wimbledon on Fridays and to Dorking market on Thursdays. His cheerful nature and saucy manner earned him friends and brought in orders. Relations and village boys helped him to plant out fifty assorted fruit trees, lay concrete, build hen-houses and pig sheds.

[ETHEL] was always working: preserving eggs in "water-glass", or pickling cabbage, damsons, onions, and eggs, and dressing fowl. bottling fruit, curing hams, carrying water from the stream for the livestock. She worked very hard, day in, day out.

[HANNAH] worked hard too, doing housework at a nearby house for 4d an hour, and calling at local houses with eggs, and produce.

[JACK] still sold greengrocery in the village; as did Bill's eldest brother [CHARLIE], while [IKE] travelled the roads as a tinker living as best as he could.

[ETHEL'S RELATIONS] were many. Some of them lived in the vicinity. frequently helping at Betchett Green, or going round to shoot rats with Bill's shotgun.

ETHEL
from a photograph

130

Disputes over wages for miners brought about a General Strike on midnight May 3rd 1926. It lasted for nine days, affecting mining, transport, heavy manufacturing, building and printing, completely disrupting life. Volunteers helped out. The coal miners stayed on strike for seven months.

In 1927 unemployment benefits became a statuatory right, and in 1930 the requirement of being "genuinely available for work" was discarded. Thus there was an immense drain upon insurance.

COPYHOLD PROPERTY was being phased out. Hannah and Bill Buckland acquired the copyhold of Betchett Green from the Duke of Norfolk in 1928

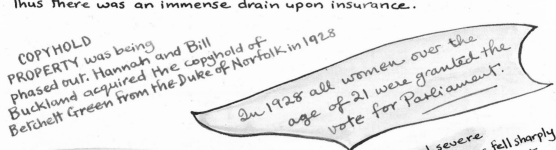

In 1928 all women over the age of 21 were granted the vote for Parliament.

SLUMP ON NEW YORK STOCK EXCHANGE VAST FORTUNES LOST BY SPECULATORS

After several severe fluctuations share prices fell sharply on the New York Stock market on 24th October 1929 Bill Buckland read about it in the newspaper, pieces of which were found fifty years later in the outside privy.

THE BUCKLAND FAMILY

Early in December 1930 Jack, who was now eighty years old, emerged from "The Holly and Laurel" public house and began to walk home; He heard a **motor car** approaching, and, seeing some of his **cattle** wandering on the road, he hastened to drive them off it.

There were about 1 million cars on the roads, but they did not pass frequently. Jack **misjudged the speed** of the car, which was travelling at about 30 miles per hour. It **hit him** and bowled him over.

He refused to see a doctor and went to his sister Hannah's. He **died** at Betchett Green a few days later.

1933
Hitler came to
power in Germany

By 1933
there was a national electricity grid with
increasingly more homes being supplied with electricity.

In Britain there
was mass unemployment,
with over 3 million out of work and
agriculture and industry both depressed.
Industry had been affected by the collapse of world
trade and by foreign competition after the war.

Ethel sent a postcard to her nephew in the army in Singapore.

POST

DORKING SURREY
24 NOV 1936 9.45 PM

Dear Bert.
Your letter just arrived
Oct 30th you wrote my
letter had just gone to
you so all I can in
time to wish you a
Merry Xmas, from us
all here no news from
homood, will answer
letter later on 24.11.36.
many thanks
9 m. Etc. ECR 13

Bill BUCKLAND sold his motor-
bike and side car, and for a
while ran an invalid car.
When motor cars became
less expensive he had a Ford
van.

Hannah was elderly, with
painful legs, but still went on
her rounds delivering eggs.
Ethel worked hard as always,
but her health was not good.

By 1937 Unemployment was reduced to 1,670,000. Unemployment in
south-eastern England had never been as serious as in northern counties.

1938   "An Astonishing Year .... Every month has been marked
          by eccentric behaviour of one kind or another".............
.... from a report in The Times on the subject of the WEATHER
January 25/26 - a brilliant display of aurora borealis lit up the night skies
and could be seen all over the country. That month there were gales too,
and in February heavy snowfalls. March and April were very dry and
mild, but there were frosts in May. An earthquake on June 11th shook
London and the Home Counties. The succeeding months saw severe heat-
waves, thunderstorms, frosts or winds, and an unusually warm November.

THE SECOND WORLD WAR
1939 ~ 1945

Britain declared war on Germany on 3rd September 1939.
after German troops invaded Poland.

Changes came very soon to people's lives, both in the towns and the country.
No bombs fell on England for several months, but children from danger areas
were evacuated to safer country places, gas masks were issued to everyone,
street lighting was extinguished, and all windows "blacked out." There were
75 summonses in 55 minutes in Dorking on 19 March 1940, against people
who had allowed light to show through their curtains. Rationing of food
was introduced in early 1940, at first for bacon, butter and sugar, then for
meat, then margerine. Cheese was in short supply and missed by farm workers.

Everything that could be repaired was saved, recycled and used
again in some form or other

In MAY 1940 prime minister Neville Chamberlain resigned and
WINSTON CHURCHILL became Prime Minister.

"You ask, What is our aim? I can answer in one word: Victory-
victory at all costs, victory in spite of terror, victory however
long and hard the road may be."

The Germans invaded Holland, Belgium and France. British exped-
itionary forces there had to be rescued from the beaches of Dunkirk
between 28 May and 3 June 1940. The beaches were bombed as the men
were taken off in every kind of boat that could be mustered to Dunkirk.
For a time some of the evacuated soldiers occupied Holmwood School, the Scout Hut, and Rover Den.

During the summer of 1940 a German invasion of England was feared.
Defences were set up and some people fled overseas. The Royal
Family stayed at Home and King George VI practised revolver shooting
in Buckingham Palace grounds, in case the Germans should arrive.

With only one leg, and being in his mid 50's, there was little that Bill Buckland could do except keep his shotgun ready. In Dorking sand bags were piled against buildings, and windows criss-crossed with tape to protect them from bomb blast. There were gun-emplacements on the Downs. Signposts had been removed so that invaders would not know where they were.

People like Bill Buckland who kept poultry could use eggs from their own fowl, but sell them only to the Ministry of Food. Those rearing animals were licenced to kill a limited number for their own use, but other animals for slaughter had to be sold to the State.

EXTRA ACRES OF LAND
WERE PLOUGHED AND PLANTED

"The Battle of Britain" began on 10th July 1940 and lasted until 15th September. The Luftwaffe attacked the south-east, the ships in the Channel, fighter bases in Kent and London. There were air fights over the south-east. Aeroplanes and bombs sometimes fell round Dorking. In August 1940 Britain began to bomb German sites, and the Germans began their "Blitz" on London and other industrial towns.

Clothes rationing began in 1941 on a points system. In the shops the clothes were marked with both the monetary price and with the number of coupons required. Farm workers, etc. received extra coupons for work clothes.

At this time Bill could buy pullets at Dorking market for £1.2s0d and day-old chicks cost 5s 0d (25p) a dozen. Rabbits were 12s0d (60p) each and calves from £1.15s0d to £4.

The Japanese attacked the American Fleet at Pearl Harbour on 7th December 1941. Germany declared war on the United States in support of Japan, and so did Italy. Now America joined in the war. The Japanese destroyed British power in the Far East and sank the battleships "The Prince of Wales" and "Repulse."

Dig for Victory   Careless talk costs lives   Don't be a Squanderbug

134

In 1942 there were shortages in the shops, coal was in short supply; there was very little building work done and there were transport difficulties.

Church bells throughout the land had been silenced, to be rung only for alarm, if there were an invasion, but on 15 November 1942 they rang out all over the land to celebrate victory against Germans in North Africa at El Alamein.

In July 1943 in Italy Mussolini's armies were overthrown by the Allied forces, and later in the year an armistice with Italy was signed.

Is your journey really necessary?
Don't take more than you can eat

135

Remember Walls have ears

"All honest people realise that trying to beat the ration is the same as trying to cheat the ration."

THE "BLACK MARKET"

Bill Buckland called regularly at Anstie Grange, which was now a training centre for officers, to collect kitchen waste for his pigs, but as time went on items for human consumption found their way from NAAFI vans into Bill's own van. He gave no coupons for any of it. He bought more and more "black market" food at Anstie and resold some of it to his relations and to other people in Holmwood and Dorking, all without coupons.

Eventually he was summoned. His customers escaped with fines of about £5 each, but Bill was sentenced to six months imprisonment. Holmwood people were shocked and Ethel and Bill's old aunt Hannah were ashamed.

Bill served his time in Wormwood Scrubs. The songwriter Ivor Novello was serving two months for using petrol for unnecessary journeys. Bill sang in the prison choir with the famous man, whose songs he had so often heard on the wireless, and had whistled while he cleaned the hen houses.

An important day in the history of the war, when Allied Forces landed in occupied France and began to push the Germans back. Meanwhile the Russians were fighting the Germans over in the east.

FLYING BOMBS, or "DOODLE-BUGS" were sent by the Germans to bomb London and the south east from the middle of June. They were pilot-less aeroplanes equipped with bombs. The drone of their engines stopped a few seconds before the bomb swished down and exploded.

THE DAILY MIRROR · 14 December 1944

10 BABY CAPITALS PLANNED FOR "VICTORY LONDON"

"Ten sleepy villages and small towns on the outskirts of Greater London may have an exciting future ahead of them." The article outlined the ideas of Professor Patrick Abercrombie for industrial satellite towns to encircle London after the war was won. Holmwood was one of the villages listed for development, but this did not take place, although other villages listed were developed.

"I'm all for it", says Mr. W.J. Buckland, of Holmwood

March 1945 — American and British Forces crossed the River Rhine — 28th April · Mussolini was executed / 30th April · Hitler committed suicide.

7th MAY 1945 GERMANY SURRENDERED.

V-E Day

VICTORY IN EUROPE DAY · 8th MAY
Everyone rejoiced

The war in the Far East against Japan still continued but the Americans decided to drop an ATOM BOMB on Japan. On 6th August 1945 they dropped the first Atom Bomb on Hiroshima, and on 9th August a second one was dropped on Nagasaki. Later in the month the JAPANESE SURRENDERED.

V-J Day

VICTORY IN JAPAN DAY · 2nd SEPTEMBER

The Second World War was Over
an evil force had been crushed.

AFTER THE WAR

1946 was a very wet year, with poor haymaking and a difficult harvest, but sugar beet, which had been grown increasingly since 1926, had the highest recorded yield in England.

THE BUCKLANDS — Bill's aunt HANNAH BUCKLAND died at the age of 87 in the Dorking Hospital, which occupied the old Union Workhouse building. She was buried at Holmwood on 8th July 1946.

Hannah left her share of the house to Bill, so that he now owned it completely.

Bill already owned three terraced houses facing the church in the village. He let them for about 8 shillings (40p) a week each, giving his tenants a rent-free week at Christmas.

1947 o FOOD was shorter than it had ever been in the wartime. Rations were cut down, and everything was difficult to come by, including housing.

The **WINTER** was very cold with heavy snow in February, (the coldest month since 1895), and March, followed by floods, and a wet April and May. The harvests for all crops were bad, and in the winter blizzards killed 6 million sheep and 30,000 cattle.

Mechanisation on farms was taking away the need for draught horses and they began to disappear from both town and countryside. In subsequent years thousands were slaughtered.

PRINCESS ELIZABETH MARRIED PRINCE PHILIP OF GREECE

bringing colour and pageantry back to Britain.

In June 1948 Holmwood people caught a glimpse of QUEEN MARY, King George VI's mother, as she was driven to Anstie Grange to attend a passing out parade. She was so impressed by the rhodo-dendron woods, which were in full bloom, that she went for a walk and was lost for a time.

Bill and Ethel Buckland made some alterations to their old house, making a small bathroom at the back of the scullery with an indoor chemical closet which could be emptied every week.

— The outside Privy —

138

In 1948 The National Health Service was established so that rich and poor alike could have free treatment from doctors, dentists and hospitals

A new era in Agriculture began, with the application of science.

Austerity was easing, with such imports as oranges and bananas appearing in shops.

The "New Look" fashion swept the country. Women cast off their plain utility skirts and wore mid-calf full skirts which required more material than the war-time designs.

Over 70% of cows were milked by hand, 30% by (rather unreliable) machines.

Cinema was very popular with everyone. Most households possessed a wireless.

Over 80% of men, and over 40% of women smoked cigarettes.

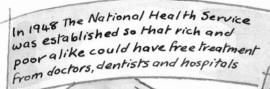

1950s

Ordinary people were better off and enjoyed a higher standard of living than they had ever known.

The decade began with the "Festival of Britain," a huge and popular fair and exhibition on the South Bank in London, and ended with the people, under prime-minister Harold Macmillan's conservative

Bill and Ethel Buckland ~ from a photograph

government believing that they had "never had it so good". Adolescents, called "teenagers" had more money to spend than ever before.

In 1953 all war-time restrictions finally came to an end, with butter, margerine, cooking fats, cheese and meat at last coming off the ration.

ELIZABETH II CROWNED 3 JUNE 1953

King George VI died in 1952 and was succeeded by his daughter Elizabeth. Her CORONATION was celebrated throughout the land with street decorations, bonfires and parties.

Many people saw the coronation in black and white on the new television sets they or their neighbours had bought specially.

1956 saw the Suez Crisis ~ a dispute with Egypt over the Canal Zone, during which, for a short period, petrol rationing again proved necessary in Britain.

After this Britain gradually began to dismantle its great and enormous Empire — countries which it had acquired and over which it had ruled since the previous century.

The Common

By the end of the 1950's Bill Buckland was one of the few people who still used the Common for livestock. The Common was changing out of all recognition. For centuries it had been acres of close-bitten grass with patches of heather, bracken, gorse and brambles.

In 1950 an eradication scheme for bovine tuberculosis was introduced nationally. This meant that Tuberculin Tested milk-producing herds of cattle could not roam amongst other animals which might be affected. In consequence all the herds of cattle which had formerly grazed freely on the Common were enclosed in fields. By 1961 people were safe from contracting the disease.

The roads encircling the Common carried traffic travelling at speed, so that creatures of any kind were in danger of being killed if they strayed onto the roads.

From 1953 rabbits began to die in their millions as the dreadful disease of myxamatosis struck them down.

Thus the bushes on the Holmwood, previously nibbled by sheep, horses, cattle or rabbits, began to grow. Thickets and trees sprang up, obscuring distant scenes that the local people had, for years, regarded as the back-cloth to their common.

Bill Buckland's poultry, scratching over the Green, were practically all that was left of the busy life that had, so short a while ago, thronged the hills and dells of the Holmwood Common.

In 1956 The Duke of Norfolk sold 630 acres of Holmwood Common to the Dorking Councils for £5,000. It was then acquired from them by The National Trust, but the rights of the commoners were unaffected.

The Scullery opening on to the lavatory and bathroom.

DRAWN FROM PHOTOGRAPHS

THE BUCKLANDS   Bill could always find something to sell and someone to buy it, even if only flowers. He sold daffodils, tulips, lilac, and gladioli. Round about the children called him "Eggy" Buckland, for eggs were his chief stock in trade. Bill's brother Charlie still had a shop in the village, and occasionally Ike would turn up: once with a particularly well-bred pony that the family believed he might have acquired illegally. Ethel's relations were frequent visitors.

Ethel, nowadays, never went away from the house, but she enjoyed seeing the people who came to the door — the boys who helped Bill to clean out the poultry pens or pick the apples, the children who called for half a dozen eggs. Some were mildly afraid of her, with her prominent pale eyes, and a beret always on her head indoors and out. She was poorly for a long time and her bed was moved downstairs. She died in the hearth room in December 1959.

Ethel Clara Rose Buckland was buried at Holmwood on 19th December 1959.

> Far from the madding crowd's
>   ignoble strife
> Their sober wishes never
>   learned to stray;
> Along the cool sequestered
>   vale of life
> They kept the noiseless tenor
>   of their way.
>
> Thomas Gray. 1716-1771

FARMERS generally were well off, as they received handsome government subsidies for all kinds of produce. HEAVY HORSES were almost an extinct species and hundreds of FARM WORKERS had also vanished as large machines requiring only one man to operate them accomplished work in a matter of hours, where previously several men with hand tools or small machines and horses had been needed.

1960's

More and more people were concerned about the possibility of a war using nuclear bombs.
BAN THE BOMB marches were held

Juvenile delinquency, crime and vandalism increased.

More married women went out to work. Divorce rates rose.

More people had indoor lavatories, bathrooms, vacuum cleaners, refrigerators, telephones, televisions, cars and holidays abroad. HIRE PURCHASE was a fast growing phenomenon.

More and more packets of frozen fruit and vegetables were being sold in the shops. Eating habits were changing

Towns were being redeveloped and multi-storey blocks of buildings were built.

THE BUCKLANDS. Bill Buckland was very lonely after Ethel died. In the summer of 1961 Bill became friendly with HELEN BEATRICE THOMAS, or BEATIE, as she was known. Beatie was middle-aged and worked as a bar-maid in The Surrey Yeoman in Dorking.

Beatie began to visit Bill at Holmwood and before long he proposed to her.

Bill Buckland married Beatrice Thomas in November 1961, much to the surprise of Bill's relations.

December 1961 was a cold month. On Christmas Eve Bill went up to the village post office; when returning home he collapsed in the lane. He was soon found and carried home, having suffered from a stroke.

On Christmas Day 1961 WILLIAM JOHN BUCKLAND died in Dorking Hospital, at the age of 73.
On a bitterly cold New Year's Day, 1962 he was buried at St. Mary Magdalene's Church, South Holmwood

142

BEATIE BUCKLAND After Bill was buried, his relations, particularly the many nephews and nieces of Ethel, were dismayed to learn that, since his marriage to Beatie, Bill had not made a new will. Ethel's relations believed that Bill had intended to leave them his property. As he died intestate everything was inherited by his wife of six weeks standing.

Beatie stayed on in the old house, keeping the chickens and selling eggs. She sold the houses in the village that Bill had owned, she sold old things out of the house to an antique dealer, and she considered selling for timber the big oak trees which surrounded the property, but a neighbour dissuaded her.

She became friendly with an ex-jockey, a Captain, who occupied a wooden Cabin in a corner of the garden. In the evenings Beatie and the Captain liked to go drinking together. Eventually they decided to marry and to buy a small business on the south coast, so Beatie began to look for a buyer for Betchett Green.

Farming

The changes in farming methods that had begun in the 1950's increased in the 60's as farmers strove to increase their productivity.

At the beginning of the 1960's chicken was still a luxury dish, although by now 100 million table birds were eaten in the year, compared with less than 5 million in the early 50's. Modern technology increased production to 260 million by the end of the 1960's.

Artificial insemination for cattle had become very popular in the late 50's for both beef and milk breeds.  Friesian cows appeared in the fields as the main milking breed and the mixed herds of former times disappeared. In 1961 the National herd was declared completely free from T.B. Also in 1961 the first Charolais cattle arrived in Britain from France, as a start towards breeding leaner beef bullocks.

Before the war farmers and cottagers had kept a few pigs of the old breeds. From 1962 there was increased interest in a scientific breeding programme for pigs, with the Landrace and Large White breeds playing a large part. Swine fever was eradicated after a campaign to stamp it out in 1963.

Sheep numbers had dropped in the 1930's due to the importation of large quantities of New Zealand lamb. The sheep population still remained low and the industry static.

Farmers were encouraged to grow corn, and new cereal varieties increased the harvest yields. Larger and larger machines were produced to harvest the crops, and as a result hedges and trees were destroyed to make larger fields to facilitate the use of the huge machines. As a consequence wild life lost habitat and the appearance of the countryside suffered. Between 1947 and 1969 hedgerows were being destroyed at a rate of 2,600 miles a year.

Artificial fertilisers, weedkillers and insecticides were used in enormous quantities, with disastrous effects upon wild flora and fauna. In 1947 nitrogen fertiliser was not in regular use on grassland, but by the 1960's it was used countrywide to increase the grass yield for grazing and for hay. Poisonous weedkillers did away with the need for weeding and for hoeing the crops, while insecticides designed to kill pests not only left residues in the crops themselves, but worked its way up the food chain of wild creatures, killing wild and game birds and foxes.

The last livestock market was held in Dorking in November 1965

In January 1965 Sir Winston Churchill died. The State Funeral was watched on television by more than half the population of the country.

So many people now owned television sets that cinema audiences dwindled and cinemas were closing everywhere. Dorking's Embassy Cinema closed in 1973.

After 149 years of habitation by members of the Buckland family Beatie Buckland sold the property in 1967 for the sum of £5,000 to

Anthony and Barbara Clark

They were a middle-aged couple with three sons. Tony Clark was a businessman who dealt with printed advertising on wrapping paper. He was over six feet tall and could not stand upright inside the house which, by now, was in a seriously dilapidated condition.

The Clarks had already had some experience in renovating a house in West Sussex, and they planned to renovate this one, despite the advice of the local council, which advised them to raze it to the ground and build a new one.

Parts of the house were in a state of near collapse, and damp rose for four feet up the walls. The garden and orchard were a jungle of elder, brambles, nettles, scrap iron and old pig and chicken pens. Even an old artificial leg which had belonged to Bill Buckland was found in the undergrowth.

A little peaceful home
Bounds all my wants and wishes; add to this
My book and friend, and this is happiness.

Francesco di Rioja.

145

There were times when the Clarks and interested neighbours expected to waken in the morning and be confronted with only a heap of rubble. One small push of the hand would make the whole house rock when the builders removed the entire front wall of the lower storey, leaving the bedrooms above supported on the timber uprights.

The old Horsham stone slabs were taken up from the earth, the floor dug out and lowered, with a concrete floor and a damp course laid. The staircases were removed and a new one made in the old scullery. The beams in the ceilings were uncovered; layers of newspapers, rushes and sheep's wool came tumbling down, together with four George III pennies.

Part of an interior wall was removed downstairs to create an L-shaped sitting room, and the fireplace was turned back into an "inglenook."

A small extension was added to make a kitchen with bath-room above, there was fresh electrical wiring, and a new cesspool dug.

By now it was 1969. Barbara Clark asked the plasterer to press into the plaster above the fireplace two pennies minted that year. In future only New Pence (decimal currency) would be minted, to be formally adopted in 1971.

Drawn from a photograph.

All brickwork and plaster was removed from the lower south wall which was propped up over a trough in preparation for concrete, a damp course and rebuilding with old bricks and breeze-block lining.

The old house was brought up to standard for modern living conditions. During the 1960's there had been a widespread rise in the standard of living, with wall to wall carpeting and central heating becoming general.

For the first time in the house's history it was no longer occupied by people who lived off its land and off the Common.

Tony and Barbara Clark turned their attention to the overgrown grounds. Barbara loved roses, but was not interested in growing vegetables. She was lavish with weedkillers. Even so brambles, elders, ash trees, dog's mercury, convolvulus and ground elder flourished. Old apple trees surrounded the house. She added rhododendrons, weeping willows and a Christmas tree fir every year she was there.

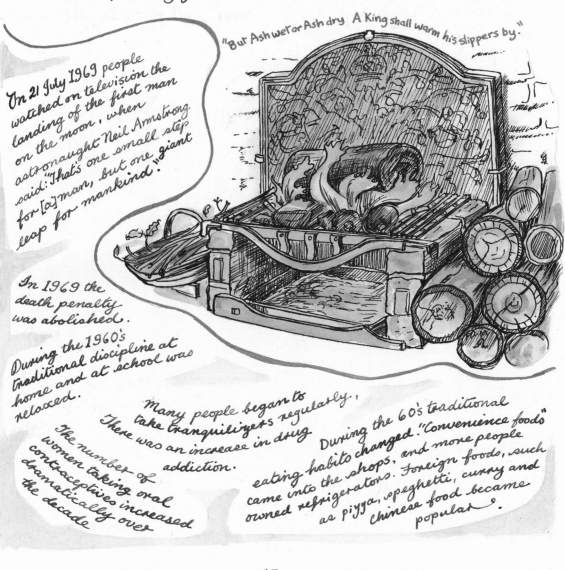

"But Ash wet or Ash dry A King shall warm his slippers by."

On 21 July 1969 people watched on television the landing of the first man on the moon, when astronaught Neil Armstrong said: "That's one small step for [a] man, but one giant leap for mankind".

In 1969 the death penalty was abolished.

During the 1960's traditional discipline at home and at school was relaxed.

Many people began to take tranquilizers regularly. There was an increase in drug addiction.

The number of women taking oral contraceptives increased dramatically over the decade

During the 60's traditional eating habits changed. "Convenience foods" came into the shops, and more people owned refrigerators. Foreign foods, such as pizza, speghetti, curry and chinese food became popular.

The Landing

Holmwood 1970. A fast dual carriageway road was being built in place of the old road between Dorking and Beare Green. It effectively cut off the main part of Holmwood Common from South Holmwood village, as to cross it on foot or on horseback was very dangerous. The village had a post office, general store, butcher's, two greengrocer's, garage, doctor's surgery, public house, Village Club, cricket team, Village Produce Association, Scouts, Guides, Women's Institute, Young Wives Group and resident policeman.

The Common

In 1965 THE COMMONS REGISTRATIONS ACT made it necessary for all occupiers who believed that rights to the local common were attached to their houses, to re-apply for rights and to prove them. The aim of the Act was to clarify which properties were entitled to rights, and exactly what those rights were. Country-wide all rights were threatened.

Barbara Clark first signed an application to register common rights on 20th May 1968. Nowadays there were only a few geese swimming on Four Wents Pond. Apart from the owners of these no one else appeared to be taking advantage of rights, and so The National Trust, which owned Holmwood Common, was surprised by a flood of applications.

By 1971 The National Trust was making matters difficult for the applicants. Some withdrew in the face of the Trust's objections, fearing that they might be involved in expence. Those Holmwood Commoners who persisted were angry and frustrated at the delays. Sharp letters passed back and forth. The Holmwood Commoners formed an Action Committee and held meetings.

It was 1972 before claims were finally registered. Only 27 properties were granted rights to Holmwood Common. Some of these had only the right of estovers, a few had piscary too, one at North Holmwood had turbary, several had the right to graze a horse.

Barbara Clark was notified that her property had the right to:

Graze 3 cows, 6 goats, 6 geese, 6 ducks and 36 fowls, with rights of pannage for 3 pigs, and to gather estovers over the whole of the Common.

The Commons Commissioner would be asked for his final consent.

Only Betchett Green and Wiggons were given the right to pasture goats, a right which had never before been the custom of the Manor, and one for which Thomas Symons, exactly 300 years before, would have been grateful.

England in 1970 to 1975

At the beginning of 1970 three quarters of the people born in Britain still lived within a mile or two of their place of birth, but during the decade many people moved further afield. The age of majority was altered from 21 to 18, giving the right to vote, to go to law, to marry without consent etc. at the younger age. Divorce on demand was permitted from 1969, and afterwards the numbers of divorces increased rapidly. There were many one-parent families.

The Women's Liberation Movement, which campaigned for women's equality with men, became strong and as a result education and relationships in the home and in working life were affected.

On 15 February 1971 the coinage officially changed over to decimal currency, however the New Pence, (popularly called "pees" rather than pennies), was already in circulation and people were becoming accustomed to it. There were frequent price rises at this time, and in 1972 a sensational increase in house prices.

In the early 70's there were frequent strikes. In January 1972 the miner's strike affected power supplies. There was a rota of times when electricity would be cut off so that people could be prepared.

1st JANUARY 1973 ∘ BRITAIN BECAME A MEMBER OF THE EUROPEAN ECONOMIC COMMUNITY, which was later to affect many aspects of life.

From 1st April 1974 the counties were re-organised, with many boundaries changed and some new counties formed with new names. This enraged many people.

DORKING MARKET

Market held on Fridays.

In 1974 the Mole-Valley District was formed for the purposes of local government. It included the towns of Dorking and Leatherhead and their outlying villages — 11 parishes in all.

The District had a population of almost 75,000 people

Dorking remained as a small town in the midst of an agricultural area. Some people commuted to work in London, others were employed in local towns, in Dorking itself, working in light industry, such as light engineering, printing and book-binding, research, etc.

The town had a few new developments of office buildings. In general the shops remained small. There were three food supermarkets and an increasing number of antique shops. Many buildings were listed as being of special historic interest, but The Red Lion Inn, scene of the old Manorial Courts had been demolished in the 1950's.

After Barbara Clark's mother died and left her a
bungalow in Hampshire the Clarks, tired of having to spend so
much time gardening, decided to move there. They did not employ an
agent but advertised the old house themselves in The Dorking Advertiser
and in The Sunday Times. Despite the house-market being almost static
in 1974 and 1975, a buyer, at £33,800 was found within two weeks.

On a hot day in July 1975 the new occupiers moved in. They were:

ALAN and FRANCES MOUNTFORD and Deutsch their Dobermann dog.

They had been living for six years in a new house only eight miles away,
but had always longed for a really old one. Originally they were both
from the West Midlands, he from Staffordshire, she from Worcestershire.
He was a foundry engineering consultant, she a part-time teacher of
exercise and dance, a free-lance writer of articles and painter of pictures.
While at Holmwood they were both to practice the sport of archery, at
which Alan became a Master Bowman.

The Summer of 1976 was glorious and memorable. The sun shone for four months and there was no rain. The Holmwood Flower Show was held as usual in July, but the flowers displayed were those normally in bloom in September. As the summer wore on plants shrivelled, the ground cracked and tap water was precious. People even re-used their bath water if possible. The leaves on big trees wilted, dried, and fell. Farmers had little grass or hay. Fire engines were busy quelling fires in forests and on heaths and commons.

A Minister for Drought was appointed by the government and not long afterwards, in late September, rain came again.

During the 1970's there was a growing awareness of the links between a good diet and a healthy body; and smoking cigarettes was linked to developing cancer.

There was a general feeling of wanting to live self sufficient lives, relying on natural sources. Some people gave up town houses for life in the country, keeping goats and chickens and growing their own food.

In 1975 the Sex Discrimination Act and Equal Opportunities Commission gave women equal rights with men.

In 1978-79 there were frequent strikes for wage settlements.

Crime rose in city streets which had formerly been safe at night.

In 1979 Margaret Thatcher became Britain's first woman Prime Minister (conservative)

Found in the orchard.

Three, four and five — leaved clovers.

1980's

By the beginning of the decade central heating had been installed in 55% of homes. 95% of families owned refrigerators and 50% owned freezers. At the old house oil-fired central heating was installed in place of bulky electric storage heaters, and the bathroom and kitchen were refitted in fashionable style, with fitted units in the kitchen.

Deep freezers made the storage of out of season foods and ready prepared meals easy, so the bottling and preserving of fruit and vegetables became unnecessary. Some farmers began to offer "pick-your-own" facilities for fruit and vegetables, many of which could be frozen at home.

At the beginning of the 1980's there was severe unemployment. By the end of 1984 more than 1 million had been out of work for over a year, but by the mid 1980's the situation improved.

In 1984 new Mole Valley District Council Offices of distinctive design were opened in Dorking.

FARMING

Surpluses of food meant that farmers must cut down on their production, so they were forced to seek other ways of making a living from their land.

Fields of rape, brilliant yellow in May, were a frequent sight, and were harvested for oil.

Some turned land into golf courses, sometimes subsidies were granted for taking land out of cultivation. Some farmers converted their traditionally built old barns and farm buildings into houses, for sale or to rent as holiday homes. The architectural alterations almost always destroyed the traditional character of the buildings.

From 1980 to 1985 hedgerows were uprooted at a rate of 4,000 miles a year and they continued to be destroyed, but generally throughout the country there was an increasing concern for the environment.

There was more interest in planting broad-leaf trees, and in growing "organic" food, i.e. without chemical fertilisers, herbicides or insectisides. Sheep became more popular than they had been for 100 years as a result of the European Common Market policies.

In 1984 more silage was made in the country than hay for the first time, after many years of perfecting a way to make it.

DEUTSCH
A strong athletic dog, with a contrary nature, a sense of humour, and a keen hunting instinct.

The **COUNTRYSIDE** around Dorking reflected the changes that were taking place in farming generally. Hedges were flayed by mechanical cutters, tubular metal gates replaced old wooden ones, plantations of young trees were planted out in pink plastic tubes to help them grow straight, clear of the weeds. Barns were converted into houses and the few farm workers that there were, were usually to be seen on enormous tractors. The numbers of riding horses increased, but beef cattle, milking cows and sheep still grazed the fields. Flocks of free-range poultry were very few. In the woods and on the commons the numbers of roe deer increased, while the rabbit population fluctuated as bouts of myxamatosis affected it.

People owned more cars and had more leisure time than ever before. Walking was popular and the footpaths well used, but traffic, even with the new motorways, was ever increasing and gave cause for concern nationwide.

April 1986 · The explosion of a nuclear power station at Chernobyl, Ukraine, resulted in radiation drifting over Europe. Radio-active fall-out contaminated pastures, affecting the marketing of sheep, especially in Wales and Cumbria.

12 January 1987. The temperature in Mole Valley, London, was -12°C had the coldest day -5°C this century.

16/17 Oct. 1987. The overnight "Hurricane" in southern England, when 15 million trees blew down in the south east. Betchett Green lost a mature oak and six apple trees, and had no electricity for two weeks.

At the old house Deutsch died at 11 years old and was succeeded by BAT, a Pharoah Hound, who had been rescued from a bad home. He was sweet-natured and gentle. His main interests in life being food, warmth and hunting rabbits.

1990s

A Birthday Present: As it approached its 400th anniversary the old house was given, in 1990, a new roof and a small single-storey extension at the back. The roof was felted for the first time and the new tiles were hand-made and uneven to blend with the house and its surroundings. Inside the extension the rear wall with its herring-bone brickwork and old timbers was retained intact as an inside wall to the new room.

The building work took from April to July and it was dry and hot the whole time.

There was a world-wide recession. In Britain many firms ceased trading. There was much unemployment, particularly in the south-east of England. There was reduced demand for many goods, including farm produce, with low prices for cereal and livestock, which made 1991 an extremely bad year for business generally.

~IN ENGLAND~

Concern was increasing for environmental, or "green", issues, which encompassed chemicals on fields and in foods, the need for re-cycling materials generally. It was felt that the country was being despoiled by new building, litter, and even tourists.

The value of breeds of plants, animals, insects, etc. which had become rare was becoming more appreciated because valuable genetic strains could be lost if they died out.

At the beginning of 1990 one in four babies was illegitimate, with many couples living together without marriage. One in three marriages ended in divorce.

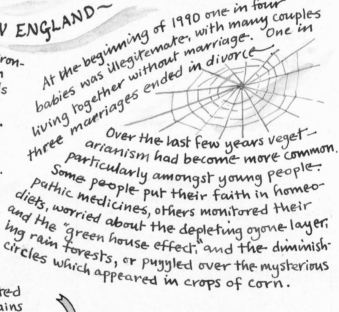

Over the last few years vegetarianism had become more common, particularly amongst young people. Some people put their faith in homeopathic medicines, others monitored their diets, worried about the depleting ozone layer, and the "green house effect", and the diminishing rain forests, or puzzled over the mysterious circles which appeared in crops of corn.

IN DORKING

in 1991 a small new shopping precinct with attractive architecture, called "St. Martin's Walk" opened near the church.

1593 - 1993

COMMENT

We had been in the house for two or three years before I began to study it properly. Six lectures on old houses opened up to me a whole new field of interest. I became fascinated by the clues to the past that the old house still contained despite alterations. I began to wonder when it had been built exactly, and then I discovered the treasures contained in Record Offices. I consulted Manorial Court Rolls, registers, minutes of meetings, maps, etc. and sometimes they held nuggets of information relevant to my search for the people who had occupied the house before me.

Eventually I came to know at least their names, and sometimes more. I calculate that about twenty babies are likely to have been born here, some of whom died when they were still small. Twelve adults have almost certainly died in the house.

Eight out of thirty-six of the occupants are known to have lived to be over eighty years of age, and ten over seventy, good ages for times when medical care was unsophisticated. Some occupants spent only a few years here, but many passed a large part of their lives, and two or three called it "home" for all of their days.

Now as I lean through the window in a summer dusk and see the bats flying, skittering across the sky and vanishing against the dark of the hedge, I wonder what Wynifreth Symons could see four hundred years ago. I watch the moving star of an aeroplane light travelling towards Gatwick. The Shute field is a large expanse of shining grass which is cut in a day for silage and in autumn cattle graze it. The wooded Redland hills can have changed only in detail, while further beyond them the woods and heaths still stretch almost to Guildford. The Holmwood Common is grown over with trees. Wynifreth would be surprised that nowadays it is mostly used only by people who walk or ride over it for pleasure. At least it is still there!

Down the garden we keep no chickens, no animals except for the dog, and we have the carp in the pond, but there are apple and plum trees, as I think there must always have been.

The hearth takes us into its embrace. This is "home", as it has been for so many, and will be, I suppose, for many more. We are here NOW, and though the past is not easy to visualise, the future is even more difficult to imagine.

COPYHOLDERS	OCCUPIERS
1593 John Symons	1593 John and Wynifreth Symons
c.1616 Thomas Symons	c.1625 Thomas and Ann Symons
1668 Thomas Symons, jnr. yeoman.	c.1662 Thomas and Sarah Symons c.1679 William and Sybilla Pilfold
1682 William Hooker, wheelwright.	
1683 James Wood, yeoman.	
1710 Richard Peters, hoopshaver.	1719 James and Sarah Peters
1743 James Peters, hoopshaver. Sarah Peters, wife.	
1765 Nathaniel Wix, poorhouse contractor.	c.1768 Thomas and Sarah Rose c.1790 James and Alice Ede
1797 Henry Marsh, yeoman.	c.1797 Henry and Mary Marsh
1800 John Tilt. yeoman.	1800 James and Martha Tilt
1805 William Bellchamber, cordwainer.	1805 William and Sarah Smith
1810 George Pannell, farmer.	1811 Mathew and Virtue Kent 1816 Edward and Jane Vaughan 1818 James and Elizabeth Buckland
1820 Mary Pannell, widow.	
1843 Charles Pannell, gentleman.	c.1846 John and Hannah Buckland
1879 Major Rhode Hawkins, architect.	1874 John (Jack) and Jane Buckland c.1880 Hannah Buckland
1920 Hannah Buckland, spinster. William Buckland, smallholder.	1916 William and Ethel Buckland
1962 Helen Beatrice Buckland, widow.	1961 Helen Beatrice Buckland
1966 Barbara Clark, wife.	1966 Anthony and Barbara Clark
1975. Alan Mountford, consulting engineer. Frances Mountford	1975 Alan and Frances Mountford.

F Mountford

SELECTED REFERENCES

Report No. 118. Domestic Buildings Research Group, Surrey.

M.S. ref MD 1203. Arundel Castle Archives.

Court Rolls of the Manor of Dorking. S.R.O

Survey 1608-1611. S.A.S. Guildford.

Survey of the Manor of Dorking with Capel 1622. S.A.S. 4/25

Copy of the Surveigh of the Manor of Dorking performed by William Forster. 1649. Copy of 1753 with extra entries. S.R.O

Dorking Parish Registers, 1538 onwards. Dorking Museum and S.R.O.

Surrey Musters 1583/4 and 1596. pub. Surrey Record Society.

Lay Subsidy Assessments for County of Surrey 1593-94. SAC. Vol. 19.

Surrey Wills. Archdeaconry Court. Herringman Register. S. Record Society.

Survey Maps of The Manor of Dorking and of Dorking Town, originally drawn in 1649. Dorking Museum.

Surrey in 1648. A.R. Michell. SAC. Vol. 67

Notes on Some Farms in Capel. H.E. Malden. S.A.C. Vol. 33

Minute Books of Dorking and Capel Quaker Meetings 1700 to 1760.

Land Tax Records S.R.O.

Dorking Vestry Minute Books, 1757 to 1799. S.R.O.

Copies of early Marriage Certificates. (courtesy of The Friends, Dorking)

Sussex and Surrey Quaker Births, Marriages and Burials Digest.

St. Mary Magdalene, Holmwood, Parish Registers. 1837 onwards.

Poor Rate Books. S.R.O

Tithe Apportionment and accompanying Map. 1841. SRO.

Minutes of the Beare Green Prosecuting Society, 1823-1890. S.RO.

Holmwood Church of England School Log Books, 1872-1962. S.R.O.

Scrap Book of Drawings, Photographs, etc of Holmwood, (courtesy St. Mary Magdalene Church).

Census Returns 1851, 1861.

International Genealogical Index for Surrey and Sussex

Bill of Sale of the Property 1914 (courtesy of Mr. M.F. Worsfold)

Medal Rolls, Archives of Ministry of Defence.

The Dorking Advertiser. 3rd, 10th March 1944, and other dates.

The Daily Mirror. 14th December 1944

Photographs c. 1916 to 1940 and Information, (courtesy Major A. Stevens).

Reminiscences of Old Holmwood, recorded by The Women's Institute, 1950's.

Will of Hannah Buckland

Photographs and Information, 1960's. (Courtesy Mr. and Mrs. A. Clark), with:

Correspondence with The National Trust relating to Commons Rights.

Papers and Records relating to Holmwood Commoners' Claims to Rights (courtesy of Mr. D. Christopherson).

Verbal Reminiscences of many Holmwood people.

SELECTED BIBLIOGRAPHY

Four Centuries of Charlwood Houses. Joan Harding. Charlwood Society. 1976.
The English Home. H.E. Priestley. Muller. 1971
The History and Antiquities of the County of Surrey. Vol.1. Owen Manning & William Bray.
The Natural History and Antiquities of the County of Surrey. Vol.IV. John Aubrey. London 1718
Life in Shakespeare's England. Compiled J. Wilson Cambridge U.P. 1911
The Elizabethans at Home. Elizabeth Burton. Secker & Warburg. 1958
Sources for the History of Houses. John H. Harvey. British Records Assn.
                    Archives and the User. No. 3. 1974
The Common Stream. Rowland Parker. Collins 1975
English Farming, Past and Present. Lord Ernle. Longmans Green, 1936
Agricultural Records AD 220-1977. J.M. Stratton & Jack Houghton Brown.
                                John Baker. 1978

The Place of Surrey in the History of England. F.J.C. Hearnshaw. MacMillan & Co. Ltd. 1936
English Country Life in the Eighteenth Century. Rosamond Bayne-Powell, Murray 1935
Everyone a Witness — The Stuart Age. White Lion Publishers. 1974
A Woman's Place. Marjorie Filbury. Ebury Press 1980
The Bax Family. Bernard Thistlethwaite. Headley Bros. 1936
A Journal of Plague Year. Daniel Defoe. O.U.P. 1969
Early Friends of Surrey and Sussex. Compiled Thomas W. Marsh. S. Harris & Co. 1886
The Georgians at Home. Elizabeth Burton. Longmans Green. 1967
Rural Crafts of England. K.S. Woods. 1945. Reprint E.P. Publishing. 1975
Victoria History of the County of Surrey. Vol.3. Ed. H.E. Malden. Univ. of London 1967
Minutes of Agriculture. Mr. Marshall. London 1778
"Causeway" - Horsham's Historical Magazine. 12 Parts. Carfax Pub. Ltd. Horsham 1970's.
Recollections of Old Dorking. Charles Rose. Reprint Kohler & Coombes. 1977
Smugglers and Smuggling. John Banks 1871. Reprint Frank Graham 1966.
Honest Thieves. F.F. Nicholls. Heinemann. 1973
The Rural World, 1780-1850. Pamela Horn. Hutchinson. 1980
Surrey Sketches in Olden Time. J.W. Kershaw. 1904
Rural Life in Victorian England. G.E. Mingay. Heinemann. 1977
Old West Surrey. Gertrude Jekyll. pub. 1904. Reprint S.R. Publishers.
Old English Sports. P.H. Ditchfield. Methuen 1891. E.P. Publishing. 1975
Folk Law and Customs of Rural England. Margaret Baker. David & Charles.
Seasons of Change. Sadie Ward. Allen and Unwin. 1982
Cuthbert Heath, Maker of Modern Lloyd's of London. Anthony Brown. David & Charles. 1980
A Short History of the Royal Sussex Regiment 1701-1926. Published 1926
Gallipoli. John Masefield. William Heinemann. 1916
English Life in the First World War. Christopher Martin. Wayland. 1974
Rights of Common and Other Prescriptive Rights. Joshua Williams. H. Sweet. 1880
The Silent Revolution. Quentin Seddon. BBC Books. 1989